FABLES: SUPER TEAM

FABLES: SUPER TEAM

FABLES CREATED BY BILL WILLINGHAM

Bill Willingham
Writer

Mark Buckingham
Steve Leialoha
Eric Shanower
Terry Moore
Andrew Pepoy
Richard Friend
Artists

Lee Loughridge
Colorist

Todd Klein
Letterer

Joao Ruas
Cover Art and Original Series Covers

SHELLY BOND
Editor – Original Series

GREGORY LOCKARD
Associate Editor – Original Series

IAN SATTLER
Director – Editorial, Special Projects and
Archival Editions

SCOTT NYBAKKEN
Editor

ROBBIN BROSTERMAN
Design Director – Books

KAREN BERGER
Senior VP – Executive Editor, Vertigo

BOB HARRAS
VP – Editor-in-Chief

DIANE NELSON
President

DAN DIDIO and **JIM LEE**
Co-Publishers

GEOFF JOHNS
Chief Creative Officer

JOHN ROOD
Executive VP – Sales, Marketing and Business
Development

AMY GENKINS
Senior VP – Business and Legal Affairs

NAIRI GARDINER
Senior VP – Finance

JEFF BOISON
VP – Publishing Operations

MARK CHIARELLO
VP – Art Direction and Design

JOHN CUNNINGHAM
VP – Marketing

TERRI CUNNINGHAM
VP – Talent Relations and Services

ALISON GILL
Senior VP – Manufacturing and Operations

DAVID HYDE
VP – Publicity

HANK KANALZ
Senior VP – Digital

JAY KOGAN
VP – Business and Legal Affairs, Publishing

JACK MAHAN
VP – Business Affairs, Talent

NICK NAPOLITANO
VP – Manufacturing Administration

SUE POHJA
VP – Book Sales

COURTNEY SIMMONS
Senior VP – Publicity

BOB WAYNE
Senior VP – Sales

This one is dedicated to my favorites of the super men: Kirby, Ditko, Romita, Kane, Kubert, Cardy, Aparo, Buscema, Steranko, Adams and Byrne.
— *Bill Willingham*

For my very own super team of Bill, Steve, Todd, Lee, Joao, Andrew, Greg, Shelly and all our wonderful guest creators who make this book a joy to work on every month. This volume is also dedicated to all the super hero books that inspired me from a very early age, especially the works of Jack Kirby.
— *Mark Buckingham*

Logo design by Brainchild Studios/NYC

FABLES: SUPER TEAM

Published by DC Comics. Cover and compilation
Copyright © 2011 Bill Willingham and DC Comics.
All Rights Reserved.

Originally published in single magazine form
as FABLES 101-107. Copyright © 2011
Bill Willingham and DC Comics.
All Rights Reserved. All characters, their
distinctive likenesses and related elements
featured in this publication are trademarks of
Bill Willingham. VERTIGO is a trademark of
DC Comics. The stories, characters and incidents
featured in this publication are entirely fictional.
DC Comics does not read or accept unsolicited
submissions of ideas, stories or artwork.

DC Comics, 1700 Broadway, New York, NY 10019
A Warner Bros. Entertainment Company.
Printed in the USA. First Printing.
ISBN: 978-1-4012-3306-8

Table of Contents

Who's Who in Fabletown 6

The Ascent 9
Pencils by Eric Shanower • Inks by Richard Friend (pages 9-10, 12)
and Andrew Pepoy (pages 11, 13-28)

Super Team
Pencils by Mark Buckingham
Chapter One: The Next Big Plan 29
Inks by Steve Leialoha
Chapter Two: Selection Day 49
Inks by Steve Leialoha
Chapter Three: F-Men! 69
Inks by Steve Leialoha (pages 69-76, 80-88) and Andrew Pepoy (pages 77-79)
Chapter Four: The Wind That Shakes the Worlds 89
Inks by Steve Leialoha (pages 89-92, 94-95, 99-103, 106-108)
and Andrew Pepoy (pages 93, 96-98, 104-105)
Chapter Five: Downfall 109
Inks by Steve Leialoha

Waking Beauty 129
Art by Terry Moore

Cover Gallery 149

Sketchbook by Mark Buckingham 156

WHO'S WHO IN FABLETOWN

BUFKIN

The reluctant but resourceful defender of Fabletown's lost business office.

FRANKIE

The remains of a certain doctor's most infamous experiment.

FLYCATCHER

The former Frog Prince and janitor, now the ruler of the Kingdom of Haven in the liberated Homelands.

BIGBY

The celebrated Big Bad Wolf and former sheriff of Fabletown.

THE NORTH WIND

Bigby's father, one of the four Great Winds.

MISTRAL

A servant of the North Win

STINKY

Now renamed Brock Blueheart in honor of the fallen Boy Blue, in whose imminent return from the dead Brock has unshakable faith.

CLARA

A cunningly disguised dragon.

KING COLE

The once and future mayor of Fabletown.

BELLFLOWER

Once known as Frau Totenkinder, she led Fabletown's witches throu their greatest trials, inclu an epic confrontation wit Mister Dark.

PINOCCHIO

Geppetto's first-carved son, transformed somewhat capriciously into an unaging boy.

OZMA

The misleadingly youthful-looking leader of Fabletown's wizards and witches.

SNOW WHITE

Fabletown's former deputy mayor, wife of Bigby, and mother to their seven cubs.

THE CUBS

Bigby and Snow's children; six are visible, one is hidden.

BEAST

Beauty's husband and the sheriff of Fabletown.

BEAUTY

The current deputy mayor, wife of Beast, and mother to their newborn.

GEPPETTO

Fabletown's former adversary, now a much-reviled fellow citizen.

ROSE RED

Snow White's sister and the leader of the non-human Fable community known as the Farm.

MISTER DARK

A Great Power imprisoned for centuries by the Adversary, he is the embodiment of all that is malign and corrupt in existence.

NURSE SPRATT

Jack Spratt's widow and an enthusiastic collaborator with Mister Dark.

THE STORY SO FAR

After seeing their beloved Fabletown laid waste and their hoarded treasures and defenses scattered, the Free Fables of the Mundane World rallied around their most powerful magical champion and mounted what they hoped would be a final assault on the elemental scourge of Mister Dark. For a brief moment it seemed that victory was theirs, but this latest adversary proved too powerful to be held for long. Soon Fabletown's survivors were obliged to retreat again — and with nowhere left to fall back to, the next stand they make against this enemy will be their last.

The Ascent

In which we take a moment to see what's been happening in the Business Office lately.

GREAT HEROES CAN'T JUST SIT ON THEIR LAURELS. THEY HAVE TO *CONTINUE* TO DO HEROIC THINGS.

WHAT'S LAURELS? IS THAT A EUPHEMISM FOR ONE'S ASS? WELL-- NOT *ASS* EXACTLY, SINCE THAT'S ITS OWN EUPHEMISM FOR BUTTOCKS.

IF SO, I GOT MY LAURELS RIPPED OFF--LITERALLY-- BY BIGBY, ALONG WITH MY *OTHER* PARTS. THAT WAS BACK IN DUBYA DUBYA TWO.

SOMETIMES I MISS NOT HAVING LAURELS. AND FEET.

AND A REAL STOMACH, SO WHISKEY DOESN'T JUST LEAK OUT THE BOTTOM OF MY NECK WHEN I DRINK.

UH--IF WE COULD GET BACK TO THE POINT...

PRECISELY!

THE POINT IS THIS: I READ ALL THE BOOKS-- BEOWULF AND GILGAMESH AND THE OTHERS. I ALREADY *KNOW* WHAT COMES NEXT.

FIRST I HEROICALLY SAVE THE DAY, THEN I'M CROWNED *KING*.

KING OF WHAT?

OF THE BUSINESS OFFICE, OF COURSE!

OFFICES HAVE KINGS? DO THE DESKS HAVE EARLS THEN, AND CHAIRS BARONS?

THIS OFFICE DOES! OR IT SHOULD! IT'S VAST AND NEVER FULLY EXPLORED.

IT COULD CONTAIN SEAS AND LOST CONTINENTS, AND BE THE BIGGEST KINGDOM EVER FOR ALL WE KNOW!

WHAT IF THERE'S ALREADY A KING?

HUH?

MAKE SENSE, FRANKIE!

IF THERE WERE ALREADY A KING, WE'D KNOW ABOUT IT BY NOW! HE'D BE HERE TELLING US TO DO STUFF!

SUCH AS GET SOME OF THESE BOOKS PUT AWAY.

WAS THAT A JAB? ARE YOU ACCUSING ME OF SHIRKING?

NO-- OF BEING A SLOB.

BUT IF THE BUSINESS OFFICE IS AS BIG AS YOU SAY, AND SO MUCH OF IT IS UNEXPLORED, THERE COULD BE ENTIRE UNDISCOVERED NATIONS OUT THERE, RIGHT?

THERE COULD ALREADY BE ONE KINGDOM, OR TWO, OR DOZENS, JUST AROUND THE CORNER.

THEY COULD ALL BE AT WAR WITH EACH OTHER, OR MAKING ALLIANCES TO COME HERE AND ADD US TO THEIR TERRITORY.

WE COULD BE DAYS AWAY FROM BEING ENSLAVED BY POWERFUL DESPOTS!

DON'T LOOK AT *ME*, MONKEY BOY. *YOU* PRONOUNCED HIM A GENIUS.

HE WAS THE FIRST TO RECOGNIZE MY *GIFTS*--WHICH WERE OBVIOUS IN HINDSIGHT.

OR IS THAT LAURELS-SIGHT?

BUT, TO GET BACK TO THE POINT ONCE AGAIN--IT'S NOT *TIME* FOR YOU TO BE KING OF THE BUSINESS OFFICE, BUFKIN.

NOT YET.

THE AGE OF BUFKIN THE GREAT HERO ISN'T OVER YET.

ONLY AFTER YOU'VE FINISHED ALL OF YOUR GREAT DEEDS DO YOU *THEN* ENTER THE AGE OF BUFKIN THE GREAT KING.

REALLY? THIS IS SOMETHING YOU KNOW? YOU'VE *FORESEEN* IT?

UHM... YEAH.

SURE.

LET'S ASSUME SO.

SO HOW MANY GREAT DEEDS **DO** I DO? WHAT'S THE OFFICIAL COUNT?

OH, I KNOW THAT ONE.

THE OFFICIAL COUNT WAS A VAMPIRE BACK IN TRANSYLVANIA. SPOKE WITH **MARBLES** IN HIS MOUTH.

I FOUGHT HIM ONCE, YEARS BEFORE I FOUGHT THE WOLF MAN. I HAD **MANY** EXCITING ADVENTURES AND SEQUELS OF MY OWN, BACK IN THE DAY.

NO, FRANKIE. HOW MANY GREAT **DEEDS** DO I HAVE TO DO? HERACLES HAD TWELVE. WHAT'S **MY** NUMBER?

THIRTEEN.

ONE MORE THAN HIM, BECAUSE YOU'RE EVEN MIGHTIER.

WELL, THAT MAKES SENSE. CAN'T ARGUE WITH THE OBVIOUS.

AND I ALREADY DID **THREE** OF THEM, RIGHT? I BOTTLED THE DJINN, KILLED BABA YAGA, AND SCOURED THE OTHER CREEPOS OUT OF THE BUSINESS OFFICE. THREE DARING DEEDS!

SURE.

YEAH.

ONLY TEN MORE TO GO.

SO WHAT'S NEXT?

MY POINT EXACTLY.

LATER...

CAN I GO?

ME TOO! I WANT A NEW ADVENTURE TOO!

NO. THIS IS MIGHTY *HEROES'* WORK. TOO *DANGEROUS* FOR WOMENFOLK.

IF YOU LET ME GO I'LL BE YOUR GIRLFRIEND.

DIDN'T YOU USED TO *RHYME?* I THOUGHT WE HAD TO TALK IN RHYME TO ASK YOU THINGS AND YOU TALKED IN RHYME TO ANSWER.

ARE *ALL* THE RULES OF CIVILIZATION BREAKING DOWN? HAVE WE BECOME *SAVAGES?*

CALM DOWN, FRANKIE.

IT WAS NEVER A REAL RULE. I JUST *PRETENDED* IT WAS A REQUIREMENT TO CUT DOWN ON MY WORKLOAD.

IF THEY DIDN'T HAVE TO PUT THINGS IN A RHYME, SOME OF MY PAST OWNERS WOULD HAVE JABBERED MY NONEXISTENT *EARS* OFF ALL DAY, EVERY DAY.

HONESTLY-- THEY WANTED EVERY LITTLE THING *REVEALED* TO THEM ALL THE DAMNED TIME.

I SEE. *SPEAKING* OF MAKING THINGS UP AS YOU GO ALONG, YOU MADE UP ALL THAT STUFF YOU JUST TOLD BUFKIN, RIGHT?

WELL, LET'S PUT IT THIS WAY, BUDDY.

I CAN TELL EVERYTHING ABOUT THE PRESENT AND THE PAST, NO MATTER *WHAT* OR WHERE, BUT I'VE NO MORE ABILITY TO SEE THE FUTURE THAN ANYONE ELSE.

SO WHY'D YOU DO IT, THEN? WHY TELL HIM HE HAS ALL THESE HEROIC *TASKS* TO COMPLETE?

DO YOU WANT BUFKIN TO BE KING OF US HERE?

WELL....

BESIDES, *SOMEONE* HAS TO FIND THE WAY OUT OF HERE AND BACK TO THE OTHER WORLDS. WHY NOT HIM?

AND YOU REALLY KNOW THE WAY?

I *SAID* I DID, SO IT HAS TO BE TRUE. I'M NOT ABLE TO LIE.

BUT IF THAT'S SO, THEN AREN'T YOU WORRIED THAT EVERYTHING YOU *TOLD* BUFKIN HAS TO BE TRUE, JUST BECAUSE YOU SAID IT?

MAYBE NOW HE REALLY *DOES* HAVE TO PERFORM THIRTEEN GREAT DEEDS AND REALLY *WILL* BECOME OUR KING AT THE END OF IT.

DID YOU CONSIDER THAT? MAYBE YOUR POWERS ARE *PRESCRIPTIVE*, AS WELL AS DESCRIPTIVE.

YOU'RE REALLY BEGINNING TO SCARE ME, FRANKIE.

I CAN'T HELP BEING A GENIUS--ALTHOUGH SOMETIMES I SUSPECT I MIGHT ACTUALLY BE A *SUPER* GENIUS.

HEY!

GRADUALLY IT BECAME CLEAR THAT BUFKIN HAD CLIMBED *ENTIRELY* OUT OF THE REALM OF THE BUSINESS OFFICE, WHERE THE PASSING OF NIGHT AND DAY WAS NEVER MARKED.

UP AND EVER UPWARDS, BUFKIN THE BRAVE ASCENDED!

HOURS PASSED, BECOMING DAYS, AS PERIODS OF DARKNESS AND LIGHT RETURNED TO THE UPPER BRANCHES.

LILY MARTAGON! YOU LITTLE *STINKER!* YOU STOWAWAY!

WHAT ARE *YOU* DOING HERE?!

I CAME ALONG TO NARRATE YOUR ADVENTURES, OF COURSE.

YOU HAVE TO GO BACK!

NO WAY! YOU *NEED* ME!

WHAT WOULD KING KONG'S ASCENT OF THE EMPIRE STATE BUILDING *BE* WITHOUT FAY WRAY? BLAND AT BEST! WORTHLESS, MORE LIKELY!

MORE IMPORTANT, WHO'D NARRATE YOUR DEEDS IF I *DIDN'T* COME ALONG?

YOU WANT TO DO YOUR DOINGS IN OBSCURITY? UNCHARTED? UNCHRONICLED? YOU'D THINK AN AVID READER LIKE YOU WOULD *KNOW* BETTER THAN THAT.

ACCORDING TO HISTORIANS, IF IT AIN'T *WRITTEN*, IT NEVER HAPPENED.

BUT YOU AREN'T WRITING. YOU'RE JUST JABBERING.

I'VE GOT AN EXCELLENT MEMORY. I'LL GET ALL OF THIS DOWN ON PAPER SOMEDAY.

SIDEKICKS ALWAYS REMEMBER THE DETAILS. THAT'S THE STORY RULE.

I'LL MAKE YOU LOOK GOOD, BOSS. *TRUST* ME.

"AND SO, CONVINCED OF THE RIGHTNESS OF HER WORDS, THE BRAVE MONKEY WARRIOR PLACED THE HAUNTINGLY *BEAUTIFUL* WOMAN BACK IN HIS POCKET AND CARRIED ON.

"THROUGH CHILLING RAIN SQUALLS!

"AND THE GLOOM OF NIGHT."

"BESET BY TERRIBLE MONSTERS!"

BACK!

BACK, I SAY--OR FEAST ON MY RAZOR-SHARP STEEL!

REALLY, FELLA, I SIMPLY INQUIRED IF YOU'D SEEN ANY GOOD *NUTS* ON THE LOWER BRANCHES. NO NEED TO ACT SO SQUIRRELY.

"NEVERTHELESS, NOT BEING A TYPICAL MALE, WISE BUFKIN WAS WILLING TO STOP AND ASK FOR *DIRECTIONS* FROM TIME TO TIME."

IF YOU GO UP HIGH ENOUGH, YOU *EVENTUALLY* FIND YOUR WAY HOME. AT LEAST THAT'S HOW THE LEGEND GOES.

HUZZAH! FABLETOWN HERE WE COME!

"HE CLIMBED UNTIL IT SEEMED CLIMBING WAS ALL HE'D EVER DONE, THROUGHOUT THE ENDLESS DAYS OF HIS LIFE."

"HE HAD RUN OUT OF FOOD LONG BEFORE AND HAD TO FORAGE FOR WHAT ODD AND EXOTIC FRUITS THE TREE PROVIDED."

AND SOMETIMES FAIRLY TASTY BUGS! REMEMBER TO WRITE THAT DOWN, TOO!

"HE LOST TRACK OF THE NUMBER OF TIMES HE'D STOPPED TO SLEEP."

SPLOOOSH!

WE'RE **SAVED!** THE TOMS ARE UNHORSED!

UNBALLED?

OKAY, THAT SOUNDS VAGUELY NAUGHTY.

WE'RE NOT OUT OF THE WOODS YET! NOT IF THAT **OTHER** TOM GETS HIS BALL BACK!

THEN WE'D BEST NOT LET THAT HAPPEN!

24

"AWAY WE WENT. AND WHEN NIGHT FELL..."

WE WERE ON ONE OF THE NOME KING'S PRESS GANGS, BUILDING A ROAD ACROSS THE DEADLY DESERT...

...LINKING OZ PROPER TO THE OTHER CONQUERED COUNTRIES.

THAT MAKES SENSE. *ROME* TAUGHT US THAT THE SECRET OF A STABLE EMPIRE IS A SYSTEM OF WELL-BUILT ROADS.

WHO'S ROME?

UHM-- DOESN'T MATTER.

WHEN WE SAW OUR CHANCE TO RUN, WE TOOK IT.

BUT THE RUMBLE TUMBLE TOMS WERE ON US RIGHT AWAY. WE'D HAVE BEEN RECAPTURED FOR SURE, HAD *YOU TWO* NOT COME ALONG.

WHAT'S YOUR PLAN NOW?

HARD TO SAY. TRUTH IS, WE REALLY DIDN'T EXPECT TO *SUCCEED* IN OUR ESCAPE.

LOOK FOR THE OTHERS WHO ARE FIGHTING BACK-- THAT'S WHAT *I'M* GOING TO DO.

DOES THIS SECRET RESISTANCE OF YOURS HAVE A *LEADER*?

WHO KNOWS? WE'RE NOT EVEN SURE IT ACTUALLY *EXISTS*.

YIPPEE!

WELL, IT DOES *NOW*.

MAKE A NOTE OF THIS, LILY. GREAT DEED NUMBER FOUR HAS *OFFICIALLY* BEGUN!

WHAT'S GREAT DEED NUMBER FOUR?

MY BOYFRIEND'S GOING TO DO THE *HERO* THING AGAIN!

THAT'S WHEN BUFKIN THE BRAVE SETS OUT WITH HIS DOUGHTY LIEUTENANTS: LILY MARTAGON, BUNGLE, SAWHORSE, AND JACK MELONHEAD--

IT'S *PUMPKIN*HEAD!

--WHATEVER--

--AND HE OVERTHROWS THE UP-START EMPEROR OF OZ, *FREEING* ITS PEOPLE FROM DIRE BONDAGE, AND PUTTING ALL OF THE MEANY TURD *STINKYHEADS* TO THE SWORD!

AND JUST WHEN DID HE DO ALL THIS?

STARTING RIGHT NOW, BOYS AND GIRLS! *RIGHT NOW!*

SO, WHO'S GOT ALL OF THE *GOOD* STUFF? THE GOLDEN CUP? THE WHATSIS BELT? THE POWDER OF LIFE? THE--

"AND THAT, DEAR READERS, IS HOW THE REVOLUTION STARTED."

NEXT: SUPER TEAM

SIX MONTHS LATER...

...NEAR ARCADIA TOWNSHIP, NEBRASKA.

HUH?

FLY?

WHAT ARE YOU DOING WAY OUT HERE IN THE ASS-END OF THE GREAT NOWHERE?

I CAME TO FETCH YOU, BIGBY.

KING COLE SAYS TO DROP THE CURRENT MISSION. IT'S *DONE*. YOU'RE NEEDED BACK IN HAVEN, RIGHT AWAY.

THE NEXT BIG PLAN
CHAPTER ONE OF *SUPER TEAM*

SO, IF YOU'RE READY I'LL BEGIN THE TEST.

THERE'LL BE SOME PROFOUND DISCOMFORT, BUT I ASSURE YOU THAT YOU'LL BE IN NO ACTUAL *DANGER* AT ANY TIME.

OH, BIGBY, YOU'RE HERE.

GOOD.

WE NEED TO GET STARTED RIGHT AWAY, SO SETTLE IN QUICK, SEE WHOMEVER YOU NEED TO SEE, AND REPORT *BACK* TO ME AS SOON AS POSSIBLE.

GOOD AFTERNOON, HIGHNESS.

DON'T WORRY ABOUT THE SUITS-- OR THE UNIFORMS--OR *WHATEVER* HE'S CALLING THEM TODAY.

I NEED TO INVESTIGATE FURTHER BUT I'M BEGINNING TO DOUBT THEY'RE AS VITAL AS PINOCCHIO *CLAIMS.* TRUST ME--WE MAY NOT NEED THEM.

WHAT WAS *THAT* ALL ABOUT?

LONG STORY. I'LL FILL YOU IN AS WE GO.

OKAY, BACK TO BUSINESS, THEN. MAYBE YOU SHOULD LIE DOWN, SO ANY *THRASHING* YOU DO WON'T BE A DANGER TO ME.

TAKE A DEEP BREATH WHILE I COUNT DOWN FROM TEN...

WE'VE GOT A BIT OF A **WALK** AHEAD OF US, BIGBY. WHAT YOU NEED TO SEE FIRST'S ON THE BORDER, AND HAVEN'S GROWN PRETTY BIG.

IT'S BECOME QUITE A HIKE FROM THE CENTER TO THE OUTSKIRTS.

I WONDER IF I SHOULD CREATE SOME SORT OF PUBLIC TRANSPORTATION SYSTEM?

HEY!

OH NO.

WAIT UP!

I WAS HOPING WE'D BE ABLE TO SLIP BY WITHOUT HIM NOTICING US.

YOU CAN'T **HOG** BIGBY ALL TO YOURSELF LIKE THAT, FLY!

I'VE BEEN WAITING TO SEE HIM FOR DAYS AND **DAYS** AND HOURS AND **HOURS** AND MINUTES AND **MINUTES!**

PINOCCHIO? WHAT HAPPENED?

WHADDAYA MEAN?

THE WHEELCHAIR.

OH, *THAT*. PAY THE CHAIR NO MIND. I DON'T NEED IT, I JUST--

WELL, YES, OF COURSE I *NEED* IT, BUT NOT BECAUSE I'M ALL PARALYZED OR NOTHING.

YA SEE, BIGGS, IT'S LIKE *THIS*. I'M IN THE CHAIR BECAUSE I'M LIKE THE *DRIVING FORCE* BEHIND THE SUPER TEAM--THE MAN BEHIND THE CURTAIN, SO TO SPEAK.

THEY'RE USUALLY ALL PROFESSOR OR DOCTOR TYPES AND ALWAYS IN A *WHEEL-CHAIR* FOR SOME REASON.

I FIGURE, IF WE'RE GOING TO *DO* THIS, WE'D BETTER STRIVE FOR AUTHENTICITY, RIGHT?

NOT A RHETORICAL QUESTION, GUYS. AM I RIGHT?

HOW SHOULD *I* KNOW? I HAVE NO IDEA WHAT YOU'RE TALKING ABOUT.

PINOCCHIO, WE DON'T HAVE TIME FOR THIS RIGHT NOW.

NO TIME? NO *TIME*?!

OLD MAN WEB IS AT A CRITICAL *STAGE* WITH BIGBY'S COSTUME!

HE'S ABOUT TO WEAVE THE INSIGNIA, SO WE HAVE TO MAKE A FINAL DECISION.

BIGBY, WOULD YOU PREFER TO GO BY *WEREWOLF MAN*--MY CHOICE--OR *BIG BAD WOLFMAN*, WHICH MAY BE MORE APT, BUT NOT NEARLY AS SUPER-HERO-Y?

Y'KNOW--IN THE *TRADITIONAL* SENSE. GOLD AND SILVER AGE, AS OPPOSED TO THE GRIM AND GRITTY ANTIHERO ERA.

I STILL HAVE NO IDEA WHAT--

PINOCCHIO, *STOP IT!*

SERIOUSLY, YOU HAVE TO STOP. THIS IS GRAVE, DANGEROUS BUSINESS.

BIGBY JUST GOT HERE AND HE HASN'T EVEN *SEEN* THE BORDER YET.

DO YOU WANT TO COME WITH US?

NO!

NOT ONLY NO, BUT *HELL* NO!

IN *NO WAY*--NO!

35

ELSEWHERE...

I HAVE TO CONFESS, MISTRAL, I'M CONFOUNDED.

A RACE? YOU'RE ON!

BUT WHAT DO WE GET IF ONE OF US *WINS*?

THIS ZEPHYR, THE CHILD NAMED *GHOST*, IS A MONSTER-- A MISTAKE OF NATURE.

IT SHOULD HAVE BEEN DESTROYED OUT OF HAND.

BUT IT'S MY SON'S CHILD. I CAN ONLY CONCLUDE HE MUST *LOVE* THE DEFORMED THING, OTHERWISE WHY NURTURE IT? WHY KEEP IT *HIDDEN* FROM ME?

KNOWING YOU'D KILL IT, IF YOU KNEW.

SO IT'S UNLIKELY HE'LL THINK ANY LESS OF YOU ONCE YOU *DO* EXTINGUISH THE MONSTER.

AT THE SAME TIME, MY SON'S MADE IT *ABUNDANTLY* CLEAR HE BEARS NO LOVE FOR ME.

MIND YOUR TONGUE, MISTRAL. BE CAREFUL HOW YOU *SPEAK* OF YOUR BETTERS.

OOPS!

SORRY, SIR. I DIDN'T THINK YOU WERE LISTENING.

I DON'T WANT TO FURTHER EXACERBATE WHAT SLIGHT *BOND* I'VE MANAGED TO FORGE WITH BIGBY. NOR DO I WISH TO POISON MY RELATIONSHIP WITH MY GRAND-CHILDREN.

IS THERE ANY WAY I CAN *FORGO* KILLING IT?

NOPE!

AT LEAST NOT HONORABLY.

I FINALLY FOUND THE VOLUME WHERE YOU WENT ON *RECORD* REGARDING ZEPHYRS.

IT WAS THAT SPEECH YOU GAVE FOLLOWING THE BIG *ZEPH HUNT*, BACK IN THE--Y'KNOW, AFTER FOGGYTOWN SUFFERED THAT CHILD MASSACRE. REMEMBER?

HERE'S THE RELEVANT QUOTE: "YOU'VE MY SOLEMN *PROMISE*, AS LONG AS I *LIVE*, NOT ONE OF THESE PREDATORY CREATURES WILL BE ALLOWED TO SURVIVE."

NOT A LOT OF WIGGLE ROOM THERE, HUH?

DAMN.

IT'S AWFUL GAUDY.

BUT I HAVE TO CONFESS, I SORT OF *LIKE* IT.

HOW CAN YOU NOT? IT'S *WICKED COOL!* A BIT RETRO, BUT WE'RE A TRADITIONAL PEOPLE.

BUT IS IT *FUNCTIONAL?* I STILL DON'T UNDERSTAND WHY SUCH COSTUMES ARE NECESSARY.

WELL, LOOK AT IT THIS WAY. YOU WANT EVERY ADVANTAGE POSSIBLE, RIGHT? AND YOU SAY THAT A LOT OF MAGIC IS BASED ON *CONFIDENCE,* RIGHT?

BELIEF MAGIC. YES, STRONG CONVICTION *DOES* CREATE POWER, BUT NOT AS MUCH AS OTHER DISCIPLINES.

SO WHAT? IF IT ONLY ADDS A *LITTLE* TO THE TOTAL, THAT'S SOME YOU WOULDN'T HAVE HAD OTHER-WISE, RIGHT? EVERY LITTLE BIT HELPS.

TRUE, BUT--

LOOK, BABE. I'M NOT AN EXPERT ON MUCH, BUT I KNOW MY *FUNNYBOOKS.* YOU'RE ALREADY PUTTING TOGETHER THE ULTIMATE STRIKE TEAM TO GO AFTER MISTER DARK.

WHY NOT MAKE IT A *SUPER* TEAM?

A SUPER TEAM *ALWAYS* BEATS THE BAD GUY! IT'S LIKE A GIANT UNBREAKABLE RULE! WHY NOT HAVE AN UNBREAK-ABLE RULE BACKED UP BY THE BELIEF OF *GENERATIONS* OF COMICS READERS IN YOUR ARSENAL?

YOU MAKE A COMPELLING POINT.

IN THE INTEREST OF FULL DISCLOSURE THOUGH, I HAVE TO WARN YOU THERE'LL BE *SETBACKS.* OUR SIDE MAY TAKE ITS LUMPS FOR A FEW ISSUES AT FIRST.

THIS IS ALWAYS WHERE YOU BEGIN TO LOSE ME. A FEW ISSUES? WHAT DOES *THAT* MEAN?

DON'T WORRY ABOUT IT. WE'VE ALREADY HAD SO MANY SETBACKS THAT WE MAY HAVE QUALIFIED FOR THOSE REQUIRE-MENTS IN ADVANCE.

SHORT VERSION IS THIS: *TRUST* ME. THIS WILL WORK.

FINE. YOU'VE CONVINCED ME.

BUT ONE THING, PINOCCHIO--

--CALL ME "BABE" AGAIN AND I'LL SHRINK YOUR ALREADY *WEE* DINGUS BEYOND ANY HOPE OF RECOVERY.

;YALP!;

MEANWHILE, IN THE CITY OF DARKLAND...

WAS THE STEAK NOT TO YOUR *TASTE*, MISS?

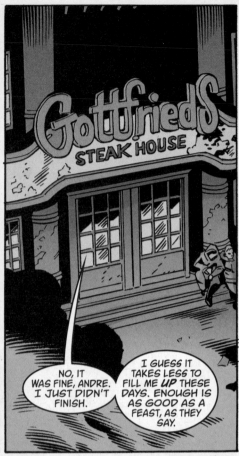

Gottfrieds STEAK HOUSE

NO, IT WAS FINE, ANDRE. I JUST DIDN'T FINISH.

I GUESS IT TAKES LESS TO FILL ME *UP* THESE DAYS. ENOUGH IS AS GOOD AS A FEAST, AS THEY SAY.

BUT FOR TOMORROW, PLEASE TELL CHEF THAT I'D LIKE A *LEANER* TRIMMED CUT, WITH LESS MARBLING. TOO MUCH FAT IN THE MEAT PUTS TOO MUCH FAT ON THE HIPS.

OF COURSE, MISS. *ANYTHING* AT ALL FOR OUR BEST CUSTOMER.

PORTRAIT OF AMERICA: AN OBESE WOMAN LEAVING A *DEATH* HOUSE, SMELLING OF MEAT AND BLOOD.

COME OVER HERE, LADY. PAY US A *MURDER* TAX. IT'S OUR WORLD TOO YOU'RE DESTROY-ING.

I'LL HAVE YOU KNOW I'VE LOST OVER A *HUNDRED POUNDS* THIS YEAR, AND CONTINUE TO DO SO.

HOW? STOPPED ORDERING THAT THIRD *BAKED POTATO*, DID YOU?

MUNDYS.

TYPICALLY *ARROGANT* IN YOUR IGNORANCE AND WORTH-LESSNESS.

I'VE MARKED YOU.

WHEN MY PATRON RETURNS FROM HIS ERRANDS, HE'LL HAVE A HARD *WORD* WITH THE TWO OF YOU, AND YOU WON'T *LIKE* IT.

NOT ONE *BIT.*

HAVEN.

NO, HONEY, IT WASN'T OUR FAULT. NO PART OF IT WAS OUR FAULT.

WE WEREN'T THERE.

WE'RE NOT THE ONES WHO THREW OURSELVES A STUPID *PARTY* WHILE MISTER DARK WAS BARELY CONTAINED IN AN OPEN COURT-YARD.

THEY DID.

THEY ACTED LIKE THE DONNER PARTY--WHICH IS UNFORTUNATELY APT--BECAUSE WE'RE *ALL* GOING TO GET EATEN FOR OUR FOLLY!

HUH? DONNER WHATSIS?

DON'T YOU REMEMBER? IT WAS BARELY A CENTURY AGO. IT WAS IN ALL THE PAPERS.

THE DONNER PARTY WAS HEADED FOR CALIFORNIA IN A WAGON TRAIN.

THERE WERE DELAYS, SO THEY WERE WORRIED ABOUT GETTING TRAPPED ON THE *WRONG* SIDE OF THE SIERRA NEVADAS BEFORE SNOW CLOSED THE PASS.

SURE, I REMEMBER THE INCIDENT. I JUST DON'T GET ITS *REFERENCE* TO US.

THEY GET IN SIGHT OF THE PASS AND ARE RELIEVED TO FIND THAT IT WAS STILL OPEN. SO WHAT DO THEY *DO?* THEY THROW A TWO-DAY *PARTY* TO CELEBRATE.

ONLY THEY DO IT WITHOUT *CROSSING* THE PASS FIRST. SO, WHILE THEY'RE PARTYING, THE SNOWS COME, THE PASS IS BLOCKED AND THEY END UP *STARVING* TO DEATH.

JUST LIKE OUR RIDICULOUS FABLETOWN *LEADERSHIP* DID, BEFORE PLACING MISTER DARK IN SOMETHING MORE SECURE THAN A HALF INCH OF GOLD PLATING.

WHAT HAPPENED TO THE PLAN TO *BOX* HIM?

IT WASN'T READY.

WHAT?

I WAS HELPING DUNSTER HAPP WITH THE NEW BOX. IT WAS STILL A GOOD TWO OR THREE WEEKS FROM BEING READY.

THAT'S NOT THE POINT!

OF COURSE IT IS, SWEETIE. THINGS DIDN'T TURN OUT FOR US, BUT NO ONE'S TO BLAME.

PARTY OR NOT, MISTER DARK WOULD HAVE ESCAPED FROM THE GOLD STATUE *BEFORE* WE HAD A BETTER CONTAINER. BAD LUCK.

I KNOW YOU WANT TO HOLD SOMEONE RESPONSIBLE, BUT THAT'S BECAUSE YOU'RE *SCARED.* I AM, TOO.

WE'LL JUST HAVE TO THINK OF SOMETHING ELSE.

IT *IS* OUR FAULT. ALL OF US, BECAUSE WE BEAT GEPPETTO AND GOT TO THINKING OF OURSELVES AS BIG, TOUGH WARRIORS.

BUT WE *AREN'T.*

WE AREN'T EXPERTS AT WAR, OR BATTLE, WE'RE EXPERTS AT *RETREAT.* THAT'S HOW WE ALL ESCAPED THE EMPIRE CENTURIES AGO.

OUT OF MILLIONS, WE FEW SURVIVED BECAUSE WE *DIDN'T* STAND TO FIGHT. WE RAN AWAY AND FOUNDED FABLETOWN. *RUNNING* IS WHAT WE'RE GOOD AT.

WE RAN FROM FABLETOWN TO THE FARM AND THEN HERE, BUT AT LONG LAST, WE'VE NOWHERE ELSE TO RUN.

THIS TIME MISTER DARK HAS *US* BOXED.

SHHHH.

YOU'LL WAKE THE BABY.

WE'LL WIN IN THE END. I DON'T KNOW HOW, BUT WE *WILL,* BECAUSE THERE'S NOT A CHANCE I'LL LET HIM GET HIS CLAWS ON YOU OR BLISS.

PROMISE?

ELSEWHERE...

NOT MUCH FARTHER NOW.

WHERE'D THE SUNSHINE GO?

IT STAYS PRETTY DARK OUT BY THE BORDERS.

WHY?

BECAUSE OF *HIM.*

HE FIRST SHOWED UP ABOUT SEVEN WEEKS AGO.

NOW HE'S ALMOST *ALWAYS* HERE--SOMEWHERE ON THE BORDER-LANDS.

B

HE'S RIGHT, BIGBY. FOR NOW I CAN KEEP HIM SAFELY OUTSIDE HAVEN, BUT IT'S HARDER TODAY THAN IT WAS YESTERDAY. AND IT WAS HARDER *YESTERDAY* THAN THE DAY BEFORE.

SSSSSSSSSS

MOST OF MY CONCENTRATION IS DEVOTED TO KEEPING THE *BARRIER* INTACT NOW.

I CAN'T AFFORD TO BE AWAY FROM HAVEN FOR MORE THAN A FEW HOURS AT A TIME.

OW!

ENOUGH!

...FOR NOW.

BUT I'LL TRY AGAIN IN A SHORT TIME, AND EVENTUALLY YOUR WALL WILL CRUMBLE!

SCAMPER AWAY, LITTLE KING, BUT SOON I'LL SEE YOU AGAIN ON *MY* TERMS.

I WANTED YOU TO SEE FOR YOURSELF WHAT WE'RE *UP* AGAINST.

I THINK YOU'RE ABOUT TO TELL ME WE'RE TRAPPED.

ESSENTIALLY, YES.

I CAN TRANSPORT ONE OR TWO AT MOST NOW, BUT AS LONG AS MOST OF MY POWER IS RESERVED TO *RESIST* HIM, I CAN NO LONGER EVACUATE AN ENTIRE POPULATION.

IF I TRY, HE'LL BE THROUGH IN AN INSTANT.

FOR BETTER OR WORSE, THIS IS WHERE WE'LL MAKE OUR LAST *STAND* AGAINST HIM.

THEN THAT'S IT. WE STAND OR FALL HERE.

WHAT'S THE PLAN?

OZMA IS ASSEMBLING A TEAM OF OUR BRIGHTEST AND BEST--OUR MOST FEARLESS AND POWERFUL--TO ATTACK AND *KILL* HIM.

FRAU TOTENKINDER PROVED WE CAN WEAR HIM DOWN, PROVIDED WE PICK JUST THE *RIGHT* ONES WHO WON'T FEED HIM POWER EVEN AS WE'RE TRYING TO DEGRADE IT.

AND YOU'VE MORE OR LESS BEEN *DRAFTED.*

NEXT: *CHOOSING THE TEAM!*

WHY THE HURRY, SNOW? THERE'S NO ONE HERE, AND WE DIDN'T *DO* ANYTHING THAT A BILLION MARRIED COUPLES HAVEN'T DONE OFTEN ENOUGH IN THE PAST.

WE HAD A VERY PLEASANT *REUNION*, AFTER BEING APART FOR SO LONG. NOTHING TO BE EMBARRASSED ABOUT.

BUT THE TREES, THEY-- THEY'RE THE *MAGIC* ONES!

MOST OF THEM STILL HAVE FACES! WHAT DID *THEY* SEE LAST NIGHT?

NOT A DAMNED THING.

PER YOUR REQUEST, I PICKED A SPOT WHERE ALL OF THEIR MUGS ARE FACING *AWAY* FROM WHERE WE DID THE DIRTY DEED.

MY JUDGMENT WAS IMPAIRED THEN BY EXTREME HORN AND THE SIXTEEN BOTTLES OF *WINE* YOU FOISTED ON ME.

AND DO THEY HAVE EARS, TOO? DID THEY *HEAR* US?

MAYBE NOT THAT MANY.

I'VE NO IDEA. WHO CARES?

WHO CARES? WELL, *I* DO, FOR--

--UH--

BIGBY?

YES, DEAR?

Uh--COULD YOU REACH UP AND GET MY *BRA* DOWN FROM OFF THAT--uhm--FELLOW'S NOSE?

I SWEAR HE HAD A SMIRK ON HIS FACE.

HE'S A *TREE.* THEY DON'T EVEN *THINK* LIKE US.

LET IT GO.

GEPPETTO.

MISS WHITE.

YOU LOOK FRUSTRATED. IS SOMETHING WRONG?

BESIDES THE FACT THAT YOUR FROG KING HAS MAGICALLY BLOCKED ME FROM EVEN *APPROACHING* MY SACRED GROVE, WHILE YOU TWO ARE ALLOWED TO CARRY ON WITHIN IT LIKE FILTHY *ANIMALS?*

LET IT GO, HONEY.

THE PEASANT KING HAS CONFINED ME FROM MY TREES, BUT HIS HOLD OVER MAGIC *WITHIN* HIS REALM IS NO LONGER AS COMPLETE AS IT WAS.

HE'S OVERBURDENED THESE DAYS. *DISTRACTED.*

MANY OF THE SMALLER DETAILS ARE SLIPPING BY HIM.

I'M READY FOR MY SACRED QUEST, HONORED EMPEROR.

GO THEN, SIR WOLDRED. MAKE YOUR WAY TO WHERE I CANNOT.

SPEAK WITH MY AUTHORITY, WHERE MY *VOICE* HAS BEEN SILENCED.

I WILL NOT FALTER IN MY DUTY, SIRE!

TRYING TO VEX ME, FROG KING, IS LIKE ATTEMPTING TO PET A VIPER.

YOU'LL HAVE ONLY *YOURSELF* TO BLAME WHEN YOU FIND YOURSELF SORE BITTEN.

DARKLAND.

ONE HUNDRED AND SEVENTY-TWO!

ANOTHER THREE AND A HALF POUNDS LOST SINCE YESTER-DAY!

SPLENDID!

I AGREE. THAT *IS* IMPRESSIVE, MADAM.

WHO--?!

YES, EXACTLY.

AS I WAS SAYING, I'M WERIAN HOLT, ESQUIRE. AS OUR MUTUAL *BENEFACTOR* PROMISED--

YOU'RE MY HANDSOME PRINCE?

AH--WELL, THANK YOU, MADAM. THAT'S *QUITE* FLATTERING.

BUT WHAT I MEANT TO SAY IS I'VE BEEN *ENGAGED*, BY MISTER DARK, TO HELP YOU ALONG ON HIS VOW TO TURN YOU INTO THE "FAIREST IN ALL THE LAND."

AS REMARKABLE AS YOUR WEIGHT LOSS HAS BEEN, AND *CONTINUES* TO BE, IT ISN'T BY ITSELF ENOUGH TO COMPLETE THE TRANSFORMATION.

YOU NEED TONE AND DEFINITION, DEAR LADY. DIET ALONE WON'T SUFFICE. IT MUST BE EVER AND ALWAYS MARRIED TO *EXERCISE* TO DO THE JOB.

THAT'S WHERE *I* COME IN.

SO--?

I'M YOUR FENCING INSTRUCTOR.

HAVEN.

KEEP GOING, WEYLAND.

I'LL FOLD MORE *MAGIC* INTO THE METAL EACH TIME YOU STRIKE.

THIS IS GOING TO BE A *MIGHTY* SUIT OF ARMOR, SIRE! TOUGHER THAN THE STRONGEST ADAMANT!

NO HARM CAN COME TO YOU WHEN YOU WEAR *THIS* INTO BATTLE!

LET'S HOPE SO, WEYLAND.

IF I CAN *CONTINUE*--uh-- YOUR HIGHNESS?

BROCK AND GRINDER ARE IN, CLARA, TOO. I'VE TESTED THEM THOROUGHLY AND THEY'RE *ENTIRELY* WITHOUT FEAR.

BEAST AND BIGBY ARE SUBSTANTIALLY THE SAME, EXCEPT--

YOU'RE NOT ABOUT TO TELL ME THAT BIGBY FEARS ANYTHING OR ANYONE. I SIMPLY CAN'T *BELIEVE* SUCH A NOTION.

HE'S FEARLESS ENOUGH ON HIS OWN, BUT HIS DEEP CONCERN OVER HIS *WIFE*, SHOULD HE FAIL AND HAVEN FALL, IS TROUBLING.

I GET IDENTICAL RESULTS FROM TESTING BEAST. HE'D BE *FINE* IF HE DIDN'T HAVE BEAUTY AND BLISS TO WORRY ABOUT.

SO WHAT DO YOU SUGGEST?

ISN'T THAT *OBVIOUS*? REMOVE SNOW, BEAUTY AND BLISS FROM DANGER. TRANSPORT THEM TO THE NORTH WIND'S CASTLE, WHERE THE CUBS ARE *ALREADY* SAFELY KEPT.

I CAN'T DO THAT.

OF COURSE YOU CAN. EVEN WITH ALL YOUR DISTRACTIONS, YOU *STILL* HAVE ENOUGH POWER TO TRANSPORT ONLY THREE SOULS.

I EXAMINED YOU MYSELF, BEFORE EVEN *APPROACHING* YOU WITH THE IDEA.

HOW *DARE* YOU TAKE IT ON YOURSELF TO POKE AND PROD ABOUT OUR *KING* WITH YOUR WITCHY WAYS?!

I NEITHER POKED NOR PRODDED, MR. SMITH. I DID IT ALL FROM A *DISTANCE* AND FLYCATCHER DIDN'T EVEN KNOW IT WAS OCCURRING.

EXACTLY MY *POINT*!

WEYLAND!

SETTLE DOWN, PLEASE.

ONE PROBLEM AT A TIME.

YOU DON'T UNDERSTAND. SINCE I CAN'T EVACUATE *EVERYONE*, IT WOULD BE UNFAIR TO SPIRIT A SELECT FEW TO SAFETY. THAT'S WHAT I MEAN BY "I CAN'T."

FAIRNESS DOESN'T ENTER INTO IT. EVERYONE WON'T HAVE SOMEONE IN THE BATTLE *WORRYING* ABOUT THEM. SNOW, BEAUTY AND HER DAUGHTER WILL.

IT'S NOT REALLY ABOUT THE SAFETY OF A FEW. I COULDN'T CARE LESS. MY *SOLE* CONCERN IS THE FEARLESSNESS OF OUR COMBATANTS.

WE CAN'T AFFORD TO *EMPOWER* MISTER DARK EVEN AS WE'RE TRYING TO WEAR HIM DOWN.

I'LL CONSIDER YOUR REQUEST, MISS OZMA.

HAVE YOU FINALIZED THE REST OF YOUR TEAM?

NEARLY.

"THE FINAL SELECTIONS AND OPEN TRYOUTS ARE TAKING PLACE TODAY."

STAY IN LINE. *TRY* TO BE PATIENT. WE CAN'T BEGIN UNTIL *OZMA* GETS HERE.

IF YOU ALREADY HAVE AN IDEA FOR YOUR SUPERHERO NAME, *SPEAK UP* WHEN YOUR TURN COMES.

WHAT THE HELL?!

I LEAVE THE ROOM FOR A MINUTE AND A *TORNADO* COMES THROUGH?!

HOW?

DID YOUR FATHER COME IN WHILE I WAS OUT OF THE ROOM? WAS HE *LOOKING* FOR SOMETHING?

Gurb!

THIS IS RIDICULOUS! I JUST CLEANED!

HUH?

WHAT THE *HELL*?!

A BIT LATER IN THE DAY...

NAME?

BONNY LAMB.

OR MAYBE BONNY LAMB *PEEP*, SINCE I'M ONE OF BO PEEP'S FLOCK.

NOT YOUR REAL NAME. YOUR *SUPERHERO* NAME.

SUPER LAMB? IS THAT ALREADY TAKEN?

NOT YET. POWERS?

I'M VERY *CUTE.*

SORRY, BUT THAT'S NOT--

LOOK, FOLKS, WE ONLY WANT *COMBAT USEFUL* POWERS!

NEXT!

AND THIS SUIT--I'M SORRY, THIS *COSTUME*--WILL EXPAND TO STILL FIT WHEN YOU CHANGE INTO YOUR BEASTLY FORM?

SO I'M TOLD.

YOU HAVEN'T TESTED IT YET?

NOT SO FAR. WANT ME TO CHECK IT NOW?

PLEASE.

OKAY, IF IT IT RIPS LIKE NORMAL CLOTHES, TELL PINOCCHIO I WAS UNDER *ORDERS.*

NNNNNNNGH!

WHAT'S WRONG?

I'M NOT SURE. I CAN'T SEEM TO--

NNNNNNNNN-NNNNNGHH!!

WHAT THE *HELL?!*

RAPUNZEL. *NOW* WE'RE GETTING SOMEWHERE!

I WANT TO CALL YOU HAIR RAISER, BUT SPELL IT LIKE RAZOR, *R-A-Z-O-R* INSTEAD! *GET IT?* IT'S LIKE A PLAY ON WORDS!

UHM-- SURE. I GUESS.

SO, SHOW US WHAT YOU CAN DO.

WHAT DO YOU MEAN?

YOU KNOW. *DO* STUFF WITH YOUR HAIR.

MOVE IT AROUND. PICK UP *GUNS* WITH A FEW STRANDS AT THE SAME TIME YOU'RE--I DON'T KNOW--PICKING A *LOCK* WITH ANOTHER ONE.

ARE YOU UNDER THE IMPRESSION THAT MY HAIR CAN MOVE ABOUT ON ITS *OWN?*

WHY WOULD YOU ASSUME *THAT?*

BECAUSE, IN THE BOOKS, *EVERY* LONG-HAIRED GIRL HAS THOSE POWERS! IT'S CANON! PART OF THE *DEAL!*

SO BASICALLY, YOU'VE BEEN WASTING MY TIME WITH NINE DIFFERENT COSTUME FITTINGS.

WAS ALL THIS A DODGE JUST TO WATCH ME *UNDRESS* SO OFTEN?

AT THE FORTRESS OF THE NORTH WIND...

BRAN THE BEAR REARED UP AND *ROARED* HIS *BATTLE* CHALLENGE!

HE SWATTED ONE SOLDIER TO THE *LEFT* AND ONE SOLDIER TO THE *RIGHT,* LEAVING SIR BLUSTER ALL ON HIS *OWN.*

SIR BLUSTER DROPPED HIS SWORD AND TURNED TO RUN AWAY, HOPING TO *LIVE* AND FIGHT ANOTHER DAY.

BUT BRAN THE BEAR HAD *OTHER* PLANS. WITH ONE LAST *SWIPE* OF HIS MIGHTY PAW, HE BROUGHT AN *END* TO BOTH THE MALICIOUS KNIGHT'S LIFE AND THIS *STORY.*

COOL!

OH, NO! THAT POOR MAN!

THE END.

READ ANOTHER ONE, GRAMPAW!

READ THE *NEXT* ONE, WHERE BRAN THE BEAR FIGHTS THE *DRAGON!*

NO, READ SOMETHING WITH *GIRLS* IN IT NEXT! THE PRETTY PRINCESS!

NO, I'M SORRY, CHILDREN, BUT WE'VE NO MORE TIME FOR STORIES TODAY. YOUR GRANDFATHER HAS IMPORTANT *DUTIES* TO ATTEND TO.

SHIT!

I MEAN SHUCKS! I *CLEARLY* SAID SHUCKS!

NO PENALTY *THIS* TIME, DARIEN. WE'LL PRESUME "SHUCKS" WAS INTENDED.

I HOPE ALL OF YOU KNOW HOW MUCH YOUR GRAND-FATHER *LOVES* YOU. I'D NEVER INTENTIONALLY HURT ANY OF YOU.

THAT MAY BE THE LAST TIME THEY'RE HAPPY WITH ME.

EXCUSE ME, LORD OF THE NORTH? DID YOU SAY SOMETHING?

NO.

NOTHING.

NEVER MIND.

HOW DOES THE SEARCH PROGRESS? HAVE YOUR FOUND THEIR BROTHER, GHOST?

NO, SIR.

WE'VE SEARCHED YOUR LANDS FAR AND WIDE. IF THE ZEPHYR CAME HERE WITH THE OTHERS, HE'S KEEPING HIS *DISTANCE* FROM THEM.

OR ELSE HE'S STILL BACK IN THE OTHER WORLD WITH HIS PARENTS.

THAT'S A POSSIBILITY. WOULD YOU LIKE ME TO--?

NO. I'LL GO.

MY SON DESERVES TO HEAR IT FROM MY OWN LIPS THAT I HAVE TO *KILL* HIS SON.

IS THIS SOME NEW ATTACK FROM MISTER DARK? IS HE SOMEHOW *DAMPENING* OUR POWERS?

I DON'T DETECT ANYTHING.

SO HE'S NOT CAUSING THIS?

NO, WHAT I MEANT IS, I DON'T DETECT *ANYTHING*. NO TRACE OF YOUR CURSE, EITHER IN ITS ORIGINAL FORM OR OUR ALTERED VERSION.

WHAT DO YOU MEAN?

I THOUGHT I WAS *QUITE* CLEAR, SHERIFF. YOU NO LONGER HAVE ANY ABILITY TO CHANGE INTO A BEAST. IT'S GONE. YOU'RE CLEAN. COMPLETELY *FREE* OF THE ANCIENT CURSE.

HOW?

I'VE NO IDEA.

CURIOUS, HMMM?

DIMINUTIVE GIRL?

NO THANKS.

MINIATURE MAIDEN?

NO WAY.

WHY ARE YOU WASTING YOUR TIME ON *NAMES?* WE NEED CAPABILITIES.

WHO *ARE* YOU, YOUNG LADY, AND WHY SHOULD WE CONSIDER *YOU* FOR THE TEAM?

I'M THUMBELINA. AND I THOUGHT I'D *ALREADY* MADE THE TEAM.

YOU HAVE.

SHE HAS.

SUPER TEAMS ALMOST *ALWAYS* HAVE ONE MINIATURE MEMBER. IT'S AN IMPORTANT *RECURRING THEME,* SO I SIGNED HER UP ON MY OWN.

YOU DON'T HAVE THE AUTHORITY.

WHAT CAN YOU *DO* FOR US?

I'M SMALL ENOUGH TO RIDE CLARA THE RAVEN. WE'LL BE A TEAM. AND HER DRAGON FLAME--HOO BOY, WE'LL BE *TOUGH!*

CLARA WILL HAVE THE SAME CAPABILITIES WITHOUT YOU *RIDING* ON HER, SO YOU AREN'T NEEDED, ARE YOU?

GET *RID* OF HER.

HOLD ON! WAIT JUST A GODDAMN *MINUTE*, OZMA!

YOU CAN'T JUST *DISMISS* HER LIKE THAT! YOU CAN'T *TREAT* PEOPLE THAT WAY!

WHY NOT? SHE'S OF NO *USE* TO US.

NONE OF THOSE STILL IN LINE ARE ANY GOOD, SO WE'RE *DONE* WITH RECRUITING.

I'VE SETTLED ON THE FINAL GROUP.

YOU CAN'T TREAT FOLKS SO CALLOUSLY, YOU LITTLE *WITCH.* THEY'RE ALL SCARED TO DEATH AND KNOW WE HAVE JUST ABOUT *ZERO* CHANCE OF BEATING THE DARK MAN, AND YET THEY *STILL* STEPPED UP TO VOLUNTEER.

EVEN IF THEY CAN'T HELP, YOU STILL NEED TO *HONOR* THEIR WILLINGNESS TO SACRIFICE.

THAT'S THE *LEAST* YOU CAN DO AND STILL BE *SLIGHTLY* HUMAN, INSTEAD OF THE LOVELESS AUTOMATON YOU'RE *TRYING* TO BE.

I WARNED YOU BEFORE ABOUT CALLING ME NAMES.

BIG DEAL! TURN ME INTO A TOAD, OR A COCKROACH, OR ANYTHING ELSE! THAT WOULD *STILL* MAKE ME A HUNNERT-THOUSAND TIMES BETTER'N YOU!

WE'RE *DONE* TALKING. GO AWAY.

INCIDENTALLY, *YOU* DIDN'T MAKE THE TEAM EITHER.

THAT'S IT, THEN!

ROLL CALL!

SUPER WITCH

CAPTAIN BLUEHEART

THE GOLDEN KNIGHT

WEREWOLF MAN

FIREBIRD

THE GREEN WITCH

TOWERING TITAN

TINY TITAN

F-MEN!

SOONER THAN ANYONE EXPECTED, FLYCATCHER'S BARRIER FELL AND THE MONSTER WAS LOOSE IN HAVEN.

YEAH, WE WANTED MORE TIME TO TRAIN, BUT WHO GETS EVERYTHING HE WANTS IN THIS LIFE?

CHAPTER THREE *of* **SUPER TEAM**

NOW!

OF COURSE OUR SIMPLE STRATEGY WAS TO **BLAST** HIM WITH EVERYTHING AT ONCE.

SOME MILITARY SCHOLAR, OR GENERAL, OR SELF-APPOINTED KNOW-IT-ALL ONCE SAID, "NO PLAN SURVIVES CONTACT WITH THE ENEMY." MAYBE THAT'S **TRUE,** IF YOU HAVE A COMPLEX AND NUANCED BATTLE PLAN. BUT IF THE IDEA IS GANG UP ON ONE GUY AND JUST KEEP **HITTING** HIM WITHOUT LETUP, UNTIL YOU WEAR HIM DOWN--WELL, IT'S HARD TO IMAGINE HOW THAT STRATEGY CAN GET ALL FUDDLED, RIGHT?

TRUST ME. IT **CAN'T.**

KILL HIM!

YEAH!

OF COURSE THERE WERE CASUALTIES.

IF *OUR* SIDE WINS, THE REST OF US AREN'T GOING TO KEEP KILLING EACH OTHER UNTIL ONLY ONE IS LEFT ALIVE.

GRINDER!

WE KNEW WE'D SUFFER LOSSES.

DON'T YOU *GET* IT, YOU BIG DUMMY? IT'S NOT EVERYONE AGAINST EVERY-ONE! IT'S EVERYONE AGAINST *YOU*!

TAKE US *IN*, CLARA! LET'S DO THAT THING WE TALKED ABOUT.

OKEY-DOKEY.

PERIOD!

PERFECT!

IF YOUR PLAN IS TO BE INSIDE OF ME, I INVITE *ALL* OF YOU TO ENTER THE DARKNESS AND SEE HOW YOU LIKE IT!

GULP

SOME OF YOU MAY HAVE TO GO DOWN IN SEVERAL *PIECES*, THOUGH!

THAT TEARS IT!

YOU'RE THE ONE GOING DOWN *NOW*, MONSTER!

WE'LL SEE!

AT LEAST THAT'S ONE OF THE WAYS I CAN IMAGINE WE *COULD* WIN THIS BATTLE.

SO MAYBE YOU SHOULDN'T BE SO QUICK TO DISMISS THUMBELINA, AND OTHERS I'VE CHOSEN, AS *USELESS*, HUH?

YEAH, IF MISTER DARK'S AT ALL LIKE US, THE "ATTACK HIS INNER EAR" THING MIGHT WORK.

MIGHT *NOT*.

WE SHOULD TRY IT, THOUGH. WE SHOULD TRY EVERYTHING WE CAN THINK OF, INCREASING THE CHANCE THAT *SOMETHING* MIGHT TURN OUT TO BE THE THING THAT DOES THE TRICK.

SO HOW DO WE MANEUVER HIM INTO TRYING TO SWALLOW YOU WHOLE?

OKAY, *THAT* GAMBIT MIGHT BE A LITTLE FARFETCHED.

AGAINST MY BETTER JUDGMENT, I HAVE TO ADMIT YOU MAKE A COMPELLING ARGUMENT. I'LL THINK IT OVER.

OKAY, BREAK'S *OVER*. LET'S GET BACK TO TRAINING.

CASTLE DARK.

GOOD PARRY! NOW PRESS YOUR COUNTER-ATTACK!

IT'S CALLED A *RIPOSTE!*

I *KNOW* WHAT IT'S CALLED!

I'M NOT *STUPID,* AND I'LL THANK YOU TO QUIT TREATING ME LIKE I *AM.*

I'M NOT TREATING YOU IN ANY WAY EXCEPT AS A *STUDENT* TO MY INSTRUCTION.

HERE. LET ME HELP YOU UP. WE'VE STILL A LONG WAY TO GO TODAY.

KEEP YOUR *HANDS* TO YOURSELF!

I'M NOT SO *FAT* I CAN'T GET UP ON MY OWN!

BRAVO!

MY TWO FAVORITE FABLES WORKING SO DILIGENTLY TOGETHER TO BRING ABOUT MY DESIRES.

IT PLEASES ME TO SEE IT.

YOU'RE HERE!

I DIDN'T KNOW YOU'D BE COMING BACK TO THE CITY TODAY!

HOW COULD I STAY AWAY? I NEEDED TO SEE FOR MYSELF WHAT PROGRESS YOU'D MADE WHILE I'VE BEEN ABOUT MY BUSINESS IN OTHER LANDS.

I TOOK A SMALL BREAK FROM MY IMPORTANT LABORS TO VISIT YOU.

LET ME LOOK AT YOU.

MARVELOUS!

IN SCANT TIME YOU'LL BE SLIM AND LOVELY, AND READY TO RECEIVE THE TENDER ATTENTIONS OF YOUR HANDSOME PRINCE.

I HAVE TO CONFESS, AT FIRST I WAS UPSET THAT MISTER HOLT WASN'T THE SUITOR YOU'D PROMISED. NOW I'M HAPPY IT WON'T BE HIM.

HE'S INFURIATING!

INSUFFERABLE!

THERE, THERE, MY DEAREST DOVE. WERIAN HOLT'S PURPOSE ISN'T TO *WOO* YOU, AND CERTAINLY NOT TO *ADD* TO YOUR COMFORT.

LIKE YOU, HIS *SOLE* FUNCTION IS TO SERVE MY *WILL*.

TRANSFORMATION IS THE MOST DIFFICULT OF ALL ENDEAVORS.

BASE METAL NEEDS THE CONSTANT *BURN* OF FIRE AND *PAIN* OF HAMMER IN THE PROCESS OF BEING FORGED INTO A BRIGHT AND DEADLY BLADE.

IF YOU'RE GOING TO BECOME ONE OF MY WEAPONS, YOU'LL SIMPLY HAVE TO ENDURE HIS VIGOROUS INSTRUCTION, AND KNOW IT'S FOR THE BEST.

I'LL TRY, BUT--

NOW, AS TO THE IDENTITY OF YOUR *PROMISED* ONE, DO YOU HONESTLY IMAGINE I'D CHOOSE ANY BUT THE *BEST* FOR YOU?

FOR ALL HIS QUALITIES, MISTER HOLT IS *FAR* FROM GOOD ENOUGH FOR THE MISTRESS OF CASTLE DARK.

AT LONG LAST, HAVE YOU STILL NOT REALIZED *WHO* I'VE IN MIND FOR YOU?

FLY!

WHUMPF!

HELP THE KING!

IS HE ALIVE?

ARE YOU *OKAY,* FLY?

I.... THINK.... SO.

THE GOLDEN ARMOR DID WHAT IT WAS *DESIGNED* TO DO--KEEP ME FROM HARM, EVEN IN THE FACE OF AN ATTACK *TERRIBLE* IN ITS FURY. GOOD MAGIC IN IT.

I'M JUST A BIT SHAKEN IS ALL.

BUT EVEN THOUGH THE ARMOR WORKED *FINE,* I'M SORRY TO ADMIT ITS DRIVER DIDN'T MEASURE UP.

I'M TOO DISTRACTED BY OTHER RESPONSIBILITIES SUCH AS SECURING THE BORDER OF HAVEN TO GIVE *FULL* ATTENTION TO LEARNING HOW TO CONTROL THE SUIT.

I CAN'T CONTINUE TO TRAIN WITH YOU AND STILL KEEP THE DARK MAN AT BAY.

TRUE. I REGISTERED A SHARP SPIKE OF *FEAR* FROM YOU JUST BEFORE GRINDER LANDED HIS LUCKY BLOW.

IF YOU MEAN A KING'S RIGHTFUL CONCERN FOR THE *SAFETY* OF HIS CHARGES, THEN--

OF *COURSE* THAT'S WHAT I MEANT. NO *CRITICISM* IS INTENDED. BUT THE REASON BEHIND YOUR WORRY DOESN'T MATTER. SUCH THINGS STILL HELP OUR ENEMY.

WE CAN'T HAVE IT. I'M SORRY, BUT WE CAN'T HAVE *YOU* ON THE TEAM, KING AMBROSE.

THAT *SUCKS!* THE GOLDEN KNIGHT WAS GOING TO BE OUR TOP *TOUGH* GUY FOR DIRECT CONTACT WITH MISTER DARK.

LOSING HIM SERIOUSLY *CRIPPLES* OUR CHANCES, OZMA.

THEN WE SHOULDN'T LOSE THE GOLDEN KNIGHT, SHOULD WE? THERE'S NO *REASON* I'M THE ONLY ONE WHO CAN LEARN TO USE THE ARMOR.

IT DOESN'T REQUIRE A SORCERER. THE MAGIC IS ALREADY BUILT INTO IT. ANY STALWART WITH A FEARLESS *HEART* MIGHT DO.

TRUE. AND SINCE THE SHERIFF MEASURED *BEST* IN THAT REGARD, BEFORE THE LOSS OF HIS POWER DISQUALIFIED HIM...

HUH?

LATER.

I'M TERRIBLY SORRY TO PUT YOU IN THIS SPOT, SHERIFF.

I'D MUCH RATHER PLACE MYSELF IN DANGER THAN FORCE ANOTHER TO GO IN MY PLACE.

I KNOW THAT, FLY. AND, FOR THE RECORD, I'M NOT BEING FORCED INTO ANYTHING--AT LEAST WITH THE EXCEPTION THAT WE'VE ALL HAD THIS CRISIS FORCED ON US.

BUT I'M HAPPY TO DO MY PART. IF SOMETHING HADN'T HAPPENED TO ROB ME OF MY OWN ABILITIES, I'D HAVE BEEN PART OF THE TEAM ALL ALONG.

WELL, I'M NOT HAPPY ABOUT ANY PART OF THIS.

YOU KNOW THIS SO-CALLED SUPER TEAM IS A SUICIDE MISSION, RIGHT? YOU ACT SO BRAVE AND MANLY, AND TALK ABOUT DUTY.

BUT NONE OF YOU IS COMING BACK ALIVE FROM A BATTLE WITH THAT THING.

THAT TERRIBLE DARK THING!

AM I WRONG?

BY ANY POSSIBLE GODS, ONE OF YOU SPEAK UP AND TELL ME I'M WRONG!

AT ABOUT THE SAME TIME...

GO AWAY?

ARE YOU *INSANE?*

I'M *NOT* ABOUT TO LET YOU OR *ANYONE* SPIRIT ME AWAY TO SAFETY WHILE YOU GO OUT TO FIGHT.

I THOUGHT BY NOW YOU'D KNOW ME *BETTER* THAN THAT.

I KNOW. YOU'RE DETERMINED TO STAND BY ME, AND I *LOVE* YOU FOR THAT.

AND IT MIGHT COMFORT YOU TO KNOW THAT, THE MOMENT OUR FIGHT ENDS, THE *MOMENT* WE FALL, MISTER DARK IS LOOSE IN HAVEN.

AND BELIEVE ME, THAT'S THE MOST CERTAIN OUT-COME.

WITH NO ONE LEFT TO STOP HIM, AND NOWHERE ELSE TO RETREAT TO, YOU WON'T SURVIVE ME BY MORE THAN AN *HOUR* OR TWO.

EVERYONE WHO'S HERE NOW DIES. BARRING A MIRACLE, THAT'S ALREADY BEEN DECIDED.

WE'VE GONE AWFULLY *SHORT* ON MIRACLES LATELY. I DON'T KNOW WHERE TO LOOK FOR ONE. DO *YOU?*

I STOPPED BELIEVING IN MIRACLES THE DAY *FLY* SHOWED UP, FLUSHED WITH ALL THAT POWER, TO SAVE BOY BLUE AT THE LAST MINUTE.

YEAH, THAT DIDN'T WORK OUT SO HOT, DID IT?

YES, WE WILL GO INTO BATTLE AGAINST MISTER DARK, FIGHT HIM *BRAVELY,* AND THEN FALTER AGAINST HIS OVER-WHELMING POWER.

I'VE ALREADY *FORESEEN* THAT MUCH.

AND THEN, JUST AS WE'RE LEFT WITHOUT *ANY* HOPE OF VICTORY, BOY BLUE WILL ARRIVE IN GLORY, AND *SMITE* THE DARK ONE.

LAST NIGHT, ASLEEP IN MY SETT, I FORESAW THAT AS WELL.

OUR LAST-SECOND MIRACLE IS ALREADY A WRITTEN FACT. *GUARANTEED.*

THANK GOODNESS OUR KIDS ARE SAFE WITH THEIR GRANDFATHER.

TOO BAD THEY'RE NOW DOOMED TO GO THROUGH LIFE MISSING *BOTH* PARENTS, RATHER THAN ONE.

YOU CAN BE A REAL *SHITHOUSE* SOMETIMES.

FINE, SNOW. CALL ME ANY NAME YOU CAN THINK OF. GET IT ALL OUT OF YOUR SYSTEM.

AND THEN GROW UP AND AGREE TO DO WHAT YOU KNOW IS RIGHT. YOUR *DUTY* AS A PARENT SUPERSEDES *ANY* RESPONSIBILITY YOU HAVE TO STAY HERE AND DIE BRAVELY WITH ME.

LET FLY TAKE YOU AWAY TO BE WITH THE CUBS.

I DON'T THINK--

HOLD ON!

NEXT: *ALL BAD THINGS!*

I--

I CAN'T.

EVERYTHING I'D PREPARED, EVERY DEADLY *THING* I'D SECRETED AWAY, WAS KEPT IN THE BUSINESS OFFICE, LOST WHEN THE WOODLAND COLLAPSED.

I THOUGHT AS MUCH. I COULD TELL FROM THE FIRST MOMENT TONIGHT THAT YOU WEREN'T STRONG ENOUGH.

OH, *DO* QUIT STRAINING AGAINST YOUR *BONDS,* SON. YOU CAN'T MOVE, BUT THAT I ALLOW IT.

MY CONTROL OVER THE WINDS IS MORE POWERFUL AND MORE SUBTLE THAN YOURS. GREATER THAN YOU COULD POSSIBLY *IMAGINE.*

SIT DOWN. WE SHOULD HAVE A FINAL FATHER-TO-SON *TALK* BEFORE I SET ABOUT MY BUSINESS.

WHAT ARE YOU DOING *OUT* SO LATE ALL DRESSED UP IN YOUR SILLY SUIT?

I *NEED* TO PRACTICE MY FLYING.

WHY? IT'S A WASTE OF POWER FOR SCANT TACTICAL ADVANTAGE.

PERHAPS, BUT PINOCCHIO SEEMS TO THINK IT'S *THEMATICALLY* IMPORTANT I FLY, AND SHOOT EYE-BEAMS AND SUCH.

SINCE HE SEEMS TO *KNOW* SO MUCH ABOUT THIS SORT OF GAMBIT, I THINK IT'S BEST TO GO ALONG WITH HIM AS MUCH AS POSSIBLE.

OKAY, BUT I THINK YOU'VE *ALL* GONE NUTS.

QUITE ROUND THE BEND.

GO AWAY, LITTLE GIRL.

WHERE WERE WE?

YOU WERE ABOUT TO TELL ME WHY YOU HAD NO CHOICE BUT TO KILL MY SON.

OH, YES.

MOST GROUNDLINGS ARE *SIMPLE* FOLK. THEY LOOK AT A GREAT KING AND SEE NOTHING BUT THE POMP AND PRIVILEGE HE ENJOYS. AND THEY *ENVY* HIM FOR THAT.

WISER MEN MIGHT INSTEAD SEE THE UNBREAKABLE *CHAINS*, FORGED BY THE TERRIBLE OBLIGATIONS AND RESPONSI- BILITIES ANY GREAT KING MUST TAKE ON.

I'M THE KING OF THE NORTH.

I *CANNOT* AND *WILL* NOT BE FORSWORN. I'M COMPELLED TO CARRY OUT MY DUTY.

NO MATTER WHO SIRES IT, MONSTERS *MUST* BE DESTROYED. THAT WAS MY ANCIENT DECREE, LONG *BEFORE* YOU EXISTED.

WHOOMPH!

DAMN.

HOW FAR OUT DID THAT OLD MAN *THROW* ME?

I UNDERSTAND WHY YOU HATE ME SO, SON.

I LEFT YOUR MOTHER TO WITHER AND *DIE* OF--WHAT DO WE CALL IT?

ABSENCE?

A *HOLE* THAT COULDN'T BE FILLED, OR SEWN SHUT, SO THAT HER VITALITY FOR LIFE SIMPLY *BLED OUT*?

MAKE NO MISTAKE, THOUGH. I *DID* LOVE HER, IN MY WAY. AND, WHILE IT LASTED, IT WAS TRUE AND *COMPLETE*.

YOU NEVER UNDERSTOOD. NEVER EVEN *TRIED*.

I UNDERSTOOD YOU WELL *ENOUGH*, OLD MAN. I WITNESSED FIRSTHAND YOUR LACK OF CHARACTER.

BUT THAT'S THE *POINT*.

WINDS CHANGE. IT'S OUR *NATURE*.

FROM TERMITE TO *TITAN*, WE'RE ALL *SLAVES* TO OUR MOST BASIC NATURE.

TODAY, FOR EXAMPLE, I ADORE MY GRANDCHILDREN, AS I HAVE DONE FOR YEARS. THERE ISN'T ANYTHING I WOULDN'T DO FOR THEM. NO *SACRIFICE* I WOULDN'T MAKE.

BUT IN ANOTHER YEAR, OR A DAY, OR A MOMENT, EVEN *THAT* COULD CHANGE. I COULD FIND MYSELF SUDDENLY *INDIFFERENT* TO THEM IN THE SPACE OF A HEARTBEAT.

TRUTH BE TOLD, I ALMOST WISH I FELT THAT WAY *NOW*, SO THAT WOUNDING THEM SO DEEPLY BY KILLING THEIR BROTHER WOULDN'T AGONIZE ME SO.

IF YOU'RE SO GODDAMN *FICKLE*, WHY NOT CHANGE INTO SOMEONE WHO DOESN'T *CARE* ABOUT THE OATHS HE'S TAKEN AND THE PROMISES HE'S MADE?

BECOME A SHIFTLESS AND *UNRELIABLE* SCOUNDREL.

I *KNOW* YOU HAVE IT IN YOU. I *SAW* IT.

BE A VERSION OF YOURSELF THAT DOESN'T FEEL THE NEED TO *EXECUTE* ONE OF MY CHILDREN, JUST TO PROVE HIS RIDICULOUS SENSE OF *HONOR*.

GOOD IDEA.

WOULD THAT I COULD SNAP MY FINGERS AND MAKE IT *SO*.

DO YOU THINK I **PLAN** THESE CHANGES OF DIRECTION?

DO YOU IMAGINE I'M THE SOLE CREATURE IN ALL OF **CREATION** WHOSE WHIMS AND MOODS ARE THE PRODUCT OF COLD DESIGN AND CALCULATION?

WHAT I IMAGINE IS, YOU'RE FULL OF **SHIT.** AND I DON'T BELIEVE A **WORD** YOU SAY.

I THINK CLAIMING YOU HAVE NO CONTROL OVER YOUR MOODS AND CORE BELIEFS IS SOMETHING YOU'VE **MADE UP** TO **EXCUSE** YOUR BAD DEEDS.

JUST LIKE EVERY **OTHER** COMMON VILLAIN. "IT'S NOT **MY** FAULT!"

IF YOU **REALLY** DON'T HAVE ANY SELF-CONTROL--JEKYLL ONE MINUTE AND HYDE THE NEXT--THEN YOU'RE, BY DEFINITION, A **MONSTER.**

AND BY YOUR **OWN** IRREVOCABLE, UNWAVERING STANDARDS, MONSTERS HAVE TO BE DESTROYED **WHEREVER** THEY'RE FOUND.

RIGHT?

SO WHY AREN'T YOU ALREADY **DEAD** BY YOUR OWN HAND?

TOUCHÉ.

WELL ARGUED.

SO WHAT ARE YOU GOING TO *DO*?

PLEASE BE QUIET. YOU NEED TO *LEARN* WHEN YOU'VE *WON*.

I NEED TO CONCENTRATE NOW, TO MAKE A CALL.

IN NEW YORK'S DARK AND UNPLEASANT LAND...

I'M SORRY, LOVE, BUT I MUST BE OFF.

I CAN'T STAY TOO LONG AWAY FROM HAVEN, WHEN I'M MAKING SUCH PROGRESS IN DEGRADING ITS WARDS.

MUST KEEP UP THE PRESSURE. SHIRKERS ARE SELDOM REWARDED.

THE FROG KING'S BARRIERS WILL FALL IN A DAY OR TWO AT THE MOST. THEN I'LL BE IN THERE RAKING AMONG THEM.

BUT YOU PROMISED ME I'D BE THERE, TO SEE THEM ALL MADE *UGLY* BEFORE THEY DIE.

AND SO YOU SHALL BE. I'LL CALL YOU TO MY SIDE THE MOMENT THE RAMPARTS FALL.

BUT THAT WON'T DO. I'M NOT *READY* YET.

I'M NOT PRETTY YET. I CAN'T HAVE THEM SEE ME LIKE THIS. STILL *FAT.* STILL *UGLY.*

YOU'RE ALREADY LOVELY TO ME, DEAREST ONE, FOR I CAN SEE WHAT YOU'RE BECOMING.

BUT NOT QUICKLY ENOUGH. CAN'T YOU SPEED THINGS UP?

NOT WITHOUT *HURTING* YOU. EVEN IN MY MOST MAGICAL OF REALMS THERE'S NO SUCH THING AS A FREE LUNCH. SUCH *LOVELY* IDIOMS THE MUNDYS HAVE.

THE PAIN OF EXERCISE AND PRIVATION THAT YOU ENDURE NOW WILL BE MULTIPLIED TO MATCH THE ACCELERATED RATE OF CHANGE.

I DON'T CARE *HOW* MUCH IT HURTS. IT'S WORTH IT.

DO IT. CHANGE ME *NOW*.

AS YOU WISH.

STEP OUT OF BED.

NO NEED TO RUIN THE GOOD LINENS. READY?

AAAAAAAARR-RRAAAGHHH!!

BACK IN HAVEN...

DESPITE YOUR ENTHUSIASM AND DETERMINATION, YOUR SILLY BAND OF WARRIORS WOULD NEVER *SURVIVE* A FIGHT WITH THE DARK ONE, ANY MORE THAN YOU COULD SURVIVE ONE WITH *ME*.

YOU THINK YOU HAVE A CHANCE BECAUSE THE OTHER WITCH DID SO *WELL*--NEARLY WORE HIM DOWN.

BUT SHE WAS SOMETHING *SPECIAL*. AND SHE SPENT ALL SHE HAD, DOING AS WELL AS SHE DID. MORE THAN A *MILLENNIUM* OF ACCUMULATED POWER.

IN THE PROCESS SHE EMPTIED HERSELF, BECOMING SMALL AND *ORDINARY*, JUST AS SHE'D REACHED THE THRESHOLD OF GREATNESS.

SHE MIGHT HAVE BEEN ON THE CUSP OF BECOMING ONE OF *US*--SOME SORT OF ARCHETYPE OF WITCHES. WHO KNOWS?

NOW IT'LL TAKE HER AT LEAST ANOTHER THOUSAND YEARS TO BECOME EVEN A *SHADOW* OF WHAT SHE ONCE WAS, LESS THAN A YEAR PAST.

THE HANDFUL OF YOU IN YOUR IMAGINARY SUPER TEAM CAN'T APPROACH A *TENTH* OF WHAT SHE ALMOST ACCOMPLISHED.

WE STILL HAVE TO *TRY*.

WE'VE NO OTHER *CHOICE*. SOME OF US TAKE OUR OBLIGATIONS *SERIOUSLY*.

YOU HAVEN'T BEEN *LISTENING* TO ME, SON.

LATER I MAY BLOW DIFFERENTLY, BUT FOR NOW I WANT ONLY THE **BEST** FOR YOUR CHILDREN.

AND IT SEEMS TO ME THEY NEED A FATHER **MORE** THAN A GRANDFATHER.

WHAT ARE YOU GETTING AT?

GO TO **SLEEP**, BOY. TAKE A GOOD LONG NAP.

SINCE THIS IS A FIGHT YOU CAN'T WIN, I'LL DO YOU ONE LAST INDIGNITY AND **ROB** YOU OF YOUR NOBLE SACRIFICE.

FEEL FREE TO SPEND A LONG TIME **HATING** ME FOR IT.

AFTERWARDS, IF I CAN, I'LL GET AROUND TO THAT **OTHER** MATTER.

NOT MY FAULT IF MORE PRESSING NEEDS INTERVENED.

I HEARD SCREAMING.

THINK NOTHING OF IT, MR. HOLT. MY INTENDED HAD AN EPISODE.

AND IT'S ONLY FIT THAT CASTLE DARK WILL BE A HOUSE OF *SCREAMS* FROM TIME TO TIME.

WHAT'S THAT?

THE SKULL OF SOME GOBLIN. I'M SAVING IT IN CASE I CAN EAT HIS TEETH LATER.

WHY NOT *NOW?*

I'D BEEN MEANING TO REMIND YOU, THE LAST OF THE CONSTRUCTION CAN'T BE COMPLETED WITHOUT YOUR WITHERLINGS.

GRANTED, BUT I'VE TEMPORARILY LOST MY TASTE FOR IT.

I'VE SUFFERED A QUEASY BELLY SINCE THE DUEL.

I WONDER IF THAT RIDICULOUS CONJURE WOMAN MANAGED TO HURT ME MORE THAN I FIRST REALIZED.

NO MIND.

I'LL RECOVER MY APPETITE IN TIME.

THE *DARKNESS* ALWAYS COMES BACK.

LOOK AFTER THINGS HERE WHILE I'M GONE, AND HANDS OFF MY *BRIDE*.

NO TROUBLES THERE, SIR. SHE'S NOT MY TYPE.

YOU SAY THAT NOW, BUT YOU HAVEN'T SEEN HER *LATELY*.

I CAN HARDLY WAIT FOR OUR WEDDING NIGHT.

CURIOUS IF SHE'S STRONG ENOUGH TO *SURVIVE* IT.

THAT'S IT, THEN.

WHAT DO WE DO WITH THE CASKET NOW?

I'M NOT SURE, BELLFLOWER. THIS IS A SITUATION *BEYOND* MY EXPERIENCE. I SUPPOSE WE SHOULD JUST LEAVE IT HERE AND GO.

I AGREE.

SO HOW DO WE DO THAT? MR. NORTH SUMMONED US HERE, BUT I'M NOT SURE WHERE HERE *IS*.

HOW DO WE GET BACK HOME AGAIN, HUSBAND?

UHM-- I'M NOT SURE.

IT'S DOWN!

WHAT?!

WHAT'S DOWN?

THE *BARRIER* PROTECTING US FROM OUTSIDERS!

IT JUST SHATTERED!

MISTER DARK IS LOOSE INSIDE HAVEN!

WE'RE AT *WAR!*

THEN--

--THAT MEANS THAT WE--

--WE ALL *DIE* NOW.

IT'S OVER.

TO ARMS! TO ARMS!

DEFEND YOUR KING AND YOUR KINGDOM!

OUT OF THE *WAY*, PEOPLE!

MAKE A HOLE!

I NEED TO GET TO THE GOLDEN ARMOR!

WAIT!

WHERE'S BIGBY?

HE LEFT EARLIER, HE--I THINK HE WENT OUT TO *FIGHT* THE THING ALONE!

WAIT! HE'S NOT HERE!

I KNOW! I JUST *SAID* THAT! I'M TRYING TO FIND OUT WHERE HE--

NO, NOT YOUR HUSBAND! *MISTER DARK* ISN'T HERE!

MISTER DARK IS GONE! COMPLETELY!

NOT EVEN A HAIR OR *WHISKER* OF HIM!

THAT--THAT'S WONDERFUL, BUT IT DOESN'T MAKE ANY SENSE.

IF THE BARRIER FINALLY CRASHED, WHY WOULD HE GO AWAY NOW?

WHY GIVE US ANY *MORE* TIME AT ALL TO PREPARE?

THAT'S THE *POINT.*

BIGBY!

WHERE--?

MISTER DARK DIDN'T GO AWAY. HE WAS *TAKEN* AWAY.

MY DAD--

I THINK MY DAD KILLED HIM.

DAYS PASS, AND THE GOOD NEWS SPREADS, IN FITS AND STARTS, AS GOOD NEWS WILL.

I MISSED HIM.

BOY BLUE CAME IN HIS GLORY, KILLED THE DARK ONE, AND LEFT.

AND I DIDN'T GET TO SEE *ANY* OF IT.

IN THE BLINK OF AN EYE.

WEREN'T THERE SUP-POSED TO BE TRUMPETS?

I DIDN'T HEAR NO TRUMPETS.

WAS IT REALLY BOY BLUE WHO DID HIM IN? I HEARD IT WAS *BIGBY*.

NOT AT ALL. IT SEEMS BIGBY WAS HIDING IN THE MAGIC WOODS THE ENTIRE TIME. APPARENTLY THE FELLOW ISN'T *NEARLY* AS BRAVE AS HIS REPUTATION WOULD SUGGEST.

IT SO HAPPENS I WAS THERE TO SEE *EVERYTHING*. IT WAS NO ONE LESS THAN *SANTA CLAUS* HIMSELF WHO DID BATTLE WITH THE DARK MAN.

YOU WERE NOT! YOU'RE *SUCH* A FIBBER! WE WERE BOTH IN THE KITCHEN GETTING WASHED! AND BESIDES, SANTA CLAUS DOESN'T *EXIST*!

HE'S A SILLY MYTH, CONCOCTED BY INEPT PARENTS TO BRIBE AND *BLUDGEON* UNRULY CHILDREN INTO BETTER BEHAVIOR.

SO THAT'S IT, THEN.

NO HEROIC SACRIFICE AGAINST IMPOSSIBLE ODDS.

NO NEED FOR A SUPER TEAM AT ALL.

AND NO NEED FOR *ME.* I THOUGHT DEFEATING MISTER DARK WAS GOING TO BE *MY* GREAT TASK-- MY JUSTIFICATION FOR TAKING OVER THE WITCHES OF THE 13TH FLOOR.

BUT IT TURNS OUT I WAS NEVER *DESTINED* TO BE PART OF IT.

WHAT'S *DESTINY* GOT TO DO WITH IT? YOU DON'T REALLY THINK EVERY-THING'S PREORDAINED, DO YOU?

I THINK THERE ARE PLANS AND POSSIBILITIES-- OPPORTUNITIES CREATED SO THAT WE CAN *RISE* TO THE OCCASION.

OR *FAIL* TO.

IF SO, THEN LET ME KNOW WHO'S *REALLY* PULLING THE STRINGS. I WANT TO *TALK* TO THAT BASTARD ABOUT MY CRAPPY-ASSED, NONEXISTENT *LOVE LIFE.*

BECAUSE, IF SOMEONE *IS* IN CHARGE, HE REALLY SEEMS TO HAVE ONE GIANT NUT AGAINST ME.

THANKS FOR AGREEING TO SEE ME.

IT SEEMS I OWE YOU AT *LEAST* THAT MUCH, CONSIDERING HOW INTIMATELY I INTERFERED IN YOUR LIFE, UNINVITED AND UNWELCOME.

STILL, YOU *DID* NEED TO GET OUT OF BED. TOO MANY FOLKS COUNTING ON YOU.

WHY? YOU MADE IT SOUND LIKE I NEEDED TO ACCOMPLISH SOME GREAT THING.

BUT I DIDN'T DO MUCH OF ANYTHING. ONCE AGAIN I WAS ON THE SIDELINES.

DO YOU *REALLY* THINK SO, ROSE?

IF YOU'D NOT STEPPED IN WHEN YOU DID, AND TAKEN CHARGE, THE FARM WOULD *NEVER* HAVE COME TOGETHER IN TIME TO EVACUATE TO HAVEN.

THE DARK ONE WOULD HAVE CAUGHT ALL OF YOU THERE, HELPLESS.

YOU SEE? *YOURS* WAS THE ONE IMPORTANT LINK IN THE CHAIN OF EVENTS THAT SAVED EVERYONE.

MAYBE SO, BUT IT *STILL* DOESN'T SEEM LIKE MUCH.

THAT'S SO OFTEN THE CASE. THE INTACT *NAIL* SELDOM GETS TO REALIZE THE VITAL ROLE HE PLAYS IN THE GRAND SCHEME OF THINGS, AND *NEVER* GETS ANY CREDIT.

IT'S THE *MISSING* NAIL THAT BRINGS ABOUT THE FALL OF GREAT KINGDOMS.

TRUST ME, ROSE RED, YOU WERE IMPORTANT, AND WILL BE AGAIN, AT LEAST *ONE* MORE TIME TO MY KNOWLEDGE.

HOW?

IT'S HARD TO SAY. HOPE ISN'T DESTINY. LEFT PASSIVE, IT'S NOTHING MORE THAN DISAPPOINTMENT *DEFERRED.* WHAT'S THAT THE MILITARY FELLOWS LOVE TO SAY?

"HOPE ISN'T A *STRATEGY.*" THEY GOT THAT MUCH RIGHT.

LACKING *CONTEXT* IT ISN'T EVEN NECESSARILY BENEVOLENT. I'M SURE MISTER DARK HAD HOPES FOR ACHIEVING MANY TERRIBLE THINGS.

SO WHAT GOOD ARE YOU, THEN?

NOT MUCH, PERHAPS. BUT I TRY TO CHAMPION THE EFFECTIVE ONES-- THOSE WHO CAN DIRECT THEIR HOPES INTO ACTIONS.

THAT'S WHY I SETTLED ON *YOU,* ROSE RED. IN THIS TIME, AMONG THESE PEOPLE, YOU'RE MY CHOSEN PALADIN.

OH, JOY. MORE RESPONSIBILITY I CAN FUMBLE.

I HOPE NOT. THE CONSEQUENCES OF FAILING NEXT TIME COULD BE *DIRE.*

HOW? IN WHAT WAY? TIME TO COUGH UP SOME *SPECIFICS,* LADY.

"HARD TO SAY. **ONE** POSSIBILITY IS THAT YOU HURT ONLY YOURSELF, AND END UP MORE OR LESS AT PEACE, RIGHT WHERE YOU THINK YOU BELONG."

ROSE
RED

BELOVED BY ALL
MAY SHE
FIND PEACE
AT LONG LAST

"OTHER POSSIBILITIES ARE MUCH WORSE."

I GUESS WE'LL HAVE TO HOPE FOR THE BEST.

SHOO! SHOO, NOW!

THIS ISN'T A TOY OR A JUNGLE GYM!

THIS IS *GLORIOUS!* COULDN'T HAVE WORKED OUT BETTER!

I HAVE TO AGREE WITH YOU THERE, KING COLE. TRUTH IS, I DIDN'T SEE ANY WAY OUT OF THIS FIX, *DESPITE* OUR DETERMINATION TO MAKE A FIGHT OF IT.

WE'LL HAVE TO START MAKING PLANS RIGHT *AWAY,* NOT ONLY TO RETURN TO THE FARM, BUT ALL THE WAY BACK TO FABLETOWN.

THIS TIME THERE'S *NO* POSSIBILITY OF THAT DARK FELLOW SHOWING UP TO SPOIL THE PARTY!

RIGHT, SNOW?

THIS TIME HE REALLY *IS* DEAD FOREVER, ISN'T THAT SO?

EXCUSE ME, FOLKS, I HAVE TO--

BIGBY? PEOPLE ARE BEGINNING TO WONDER WHERE YOU ARE. YOU'RE THE ONLY ONE *NOT* HAPPY--OR AT LEAST RELIEVED--AT THE WAY THINGS TURNED OUT.

WHY'D HE DO IT, SNOW?

I HATED HIM FOR SO LONG. I WAS *RESIGNED* TO HAVING NO FATHER--COMFORT-ABLE WITH IT.

WHY'D HE HAVE TO DO SOMETHING SO *NOBLE?*

I DON'T KNOW, SWEETIE. I'M CONFLICTED, TOO. AT THE SAME TIME I'M SO SORRY TO *LOSE* HIM, I CAN'T HIDE MY PRIDE IN WHAT HE DID.

I CAN'T PRETEND NOT TO FEEL SUCH OVER-WHELMING *JOY* AT OUR REPRIEVE.

HE SAID IT WAS FOR THE CUBS. I THINK HE REALLY DID LOVE THEM.

I FULLY BELIEVE HE DID. MAYBE IT WAS THE ONE AREA WHERE HE WAS CONSTANT. UNCHANGING.

AH, *THERE* YOU ARE, BIGBY, SON OF BOREAS, THE MIGHTY BLOWHARD, THE DEVOURING ONE.

THE NORTH WIND IS *DEAD,* AND WE MUST MOURN HIS PASSING. BUT AFTER A SUITABLE TIME, WE MUST ALSO BE ABOUT THE BUSINESS OF CHOOSING HIS *SUCCESSOR.*

AFTER ALL, THE WORLDS CAN'T BE ABSENT A NORTH WIND. THE *NEW* ONE WILL OF COURSE BE DRAWN FROM HIS BLOODLINE.

HUH?

YOU EXPECT *BIGBY* TO BE THE NEW NORTH WIND?!

DON'T BE DAFT. HE'S *ENTIRELY* UNSUITABLE.

NO, WE'LL HAVE TO MAKE OUR CHOICE FROM AMONG YOUR *CHILDREN,* OF COURSE.

NEXT: THE SLEEPING CITY

It was when the Imperial City, of the Old Empire, was officially renamed The Sleeping City (though, truth be told, the locals had called it that for years).

PRINCE LINDWORM OF SCANDA!

It was a time of multiple Emperors sans empire. Fresh ones were springing up nearly every day, proclaiming themselves the rightful new lord of lords.

I MARK YOU A *FALSE* EMPEROR AND AN UPSTART!

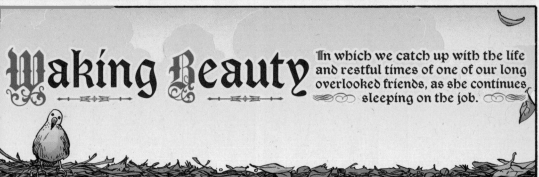

Waking Beauty

In which we catch up with the life and restful times of one of our long overlooked friends, as she continues sleeping on the job.

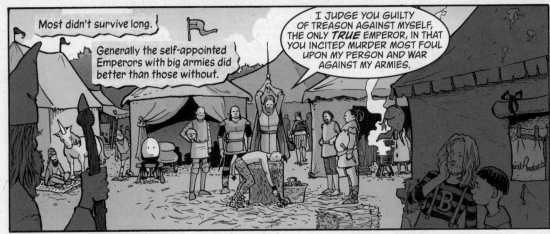

Most didn't survive long.

Generally the self-appointed Emperors with big armies did better than those without.

I JUDGE YOU GUILTY OF TREASON AGAINST MYSELF, THE ONLY *TRUE* EMPEROR, IN THAT YOU INCITED MURDER MOST FOUL UPON MY PERSON AND WAR AGAINST MY ARMIES.

THE SENTENCE IS *DEATH*.

NICELY DONE, GENERAL MIRANT.

ONE GOOD, CLEAN STROKE. THE UPSTART COULDN'T *WISH* FOR BETTER THAN THAT.

LET THE WORD GO OUT THAT A *SIMILAR* FATE AWAITS ANY OTHER PRETENDER TO THE IMPERIAL THRONE!

YOUR GUESTS ARE ASSEMBLED ON THE WESTERN LAWN, EMPEROR, AS YOU ORDERED. THEY *AWAIT* YOUR PLEASURE.

SPLENDID. LET'S GET RIGHT TO IT, SHALL WE, SERGEANT?

FATHERS AND SONS, PAY **HEED!**

I AM *JUBILEE MIRANT*, FIRST EMPEROR OF THE RESTORED EMPIRE! YOU ARE MY SUBJECTS GATHERED FROM THROUGHOUT THIS WORLD, AND *THIS* IS YOUR DAY OF GLORY!

KNEEL BEFORE ME!

AS OF NOW, ALL YOU FATHERS ARE MADE *KINGS,* SUBJECT TO ME. IN TIME, AS WE RECONQUER LOST LANDS, WE'LL FIND ACTUAL *KINGDOMS* FOR YOU TO RULE.

TODAY YOU'VE BEEN CHOSEN FOR ENLARGEMENT DUE TO THE NATURE OF YOUR HANDSOME SONS, WHO ARE NOW MADE *PRINCES.*

RISE UP AGAIN!

YOU NEW KINGS CAN NOW GO ENJOY THE BANQUET WE'VE PREPARED FOR YOU! YOU NEW PRINCES, LINE UP AND FOLLOW ME TO A FEAST OF A *DIFFERENT* SORT!

133

CONFOUND IT!

MORE THAN A HUNDRED NEW PRINCES, EACH ONE AS HANDSOME AS ANY GIRL COULD WISH FOR, AND *STILL* NO SUCCESS!

WHAT'S IT GOING TO *TAKE* TO COAX A LITTLE TRUE LOVE FROM JUST ONE OUT OF SO MANY?

OH, SPEAK *UP*, SERGEANT.

WHEN YOU PRUNE YOUR FACE AT ME LIKE THAT, I *KNOW* YOU'VE GOT SOMETHING TO SAY.

BEGGING YOUR PARDON, SIR. IT'S HARDLY MY PLACE, BUT--

SPEAK *PLAIN*, OLD CAMPAIGNER. THERE'S NO ONE ELSE HERE TO EMBARRASS ME.

IF I WERE GOING TO HAVE YOUR HEAD LOPPED OFF FOR CRITICIZING YOUR BETTERS, I'D HAVE DONE IT *YEARS* AGO.

WELL, SIR...

...IT'S JUST THAT I THINK YOU'RE GOING ABOUT IT ALL *WRONG*.

OH?

THE PROBLEM WITH THESE NEW PRINCES IS THEY'RE *NEW* PRINCES.

THEY WON'T BE THINKING ABOUT LOVE AND MARRIAGE AND SUCH-- NOT ON THE SAME DAY THEY'VE BEEN SO ENLARGED.

I'D SUSPECT INSTEAD THAT THEIR MINDS ARE ALL AWHIRL WITH THE POMP AND *ADVENTURE* OF THEIR SUDDENLY TRANSFORMED LIVES.

I DON'T KNOW ABOUT THE HIGH AFFAIRS OF KINGS AND EMPIRES, BUT I KNOW THE WAYS OF ORDINARY MEN. I'VE SPENT A LIFETIME TURNING BOYS INTO SOLDIERS.

Y'SEE, SIR, I THINK YOU WERE WRONG TODAY. I THINK YOU *CAN* MANUFACTURE TRUE LOVE--OR AT LEAST DRUM IT INTO THESE FELLERS.

LET ME TAKE OVER THEIR TRAINING. I'LL ROUST THEM EVERY MORNING BEFORE FIRST SUN, WORK THEM ALL DAY, AND RETURN THEM *EXHAUSTED* TO THEIR COTS EACH NIGHT.

AND I'LL ISOLATE THEM FROM THE FAIRER SEX.

NEVER SO MUCH AS A LOCAL MILKMAID WILL THEY SEE.

THEN, IN A FEW WEEKS, WE'LL START BEDDING THEM DOWN IN THE CITY COURTYARD, IN *SIGHT* OF THE SLEEPING BEAUTY.

BUT, FROM NOW ON, IT'S STRICTLY *LOOK* BUT DON'T TOUCH.

GENTLY NOW.

Meanwhile...

QUIET NIGHT TONIGHT.

GOOD, SERGEANT, BUT IT WON'T LAST.

AN ARMY INACTIVE TOO LONG GETS *RESTLESS*.

THEY NEED AN *ENEMY* TO MARCH AGAINST AND FIGHT SOON, OR THEY'LL LOSE DISCIPLINE.

I WANT YOU TO SET YOUR SCHEME IN MOTION *IMMEDIATELY*. LET'S GET OUR SLEEPING BEAUTY WOKEN AS SOON AS POSSIBLE.

WE NEED TO RECOVER OUR *SNOOZING EXPERTS* FROM THE OLD EMPIRE WHO CAN START THE PROCESS OF REOPENING THE WORLD GATEWAYS.

AND THEN GET *AWAY* FROM THIS PLACE, BACK ON THE ROAD OF CONQUEST.

VERY GOOD, SIR. IF THERE'S NOTHING ELSE THEN, I'LL TURN IN TO GET AN EARLY START IN THE MORNING.

Elsewhere, at another, more humble encampment...

START STRIKING THE CAMP. PACK UP.

THEY'LL BE BACK SOON.

HERE THEY COME NOW!

EXCELLENT WORK!

WERE YOU SPOTTED? FOLLOWED?

OF COURSE NOT, COMMANDER.

GOOD. PROP UP THE BODY.

PUT THE PRINCE'S HEAD BACK IN PLACE.

CAREFUL NOW, YOU GOBS! Y'AREN'T LOWERING MEAT INTO A STEWPOT!

HERE THEY ARE *NOW*, SIR!

GOOD! GRAND! LOAD HER INTO THE WAGON AND LET'S BE OFF!

ONE PROBLEM, SIR.

WE SEEM TO HAVE ONE TOO *MANY* SLEEPING BEAUTIES.

THEY WERE BOTH LOVELY AND BOTH SLEEPING IN AN OPULENT SETTING, LORD.

WE COULDN'T BE *ENTIRELY* CERTAIN WHICH WAS THE RIGHT ONE.

NEVER MIND, SOLDIER, YOU USED YOUR HEAD AND BROUGHT *BOTH*.

WE DON'T REALLY NEED TO FIGURE OUT WHICH IS WHICH, AS LONG AS TRUE LOVE'S KISS NEVER WAKES *EITHER* OF THEM.

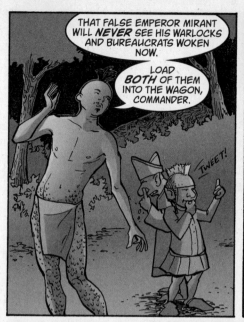

THAT FALSE EMPEROR MIRANT WILL *NEVER* SEE HIS WARLOCKS AND BUREAUCRATS WOKEN NOW.

LOAD *BOTH* OF THEM INTO THE WAGON, COMMANDER.

TWEET!

THEY'RE EACH NAUGHT BUT A FRAIL SLIP, AND BOTH CAN RIDE AS COMFORTABLY AS ONE.

AYE, EMPEROR LINDWORM.

So two beauties, rather than one, were stolen away that day. Let me tell you *that* turned into a grand misadventure.

MOVE OUT!

DID YOU TAKE CARE OF THAT *OTHER* MATTER, SOLDIER?

YES INDEED, COMMANDER.

IT'S NO USE, SIR. THE CITY'S LOST.

AND THE SLEEPING BEAUTY?

NO WAY TO TELL. THE FLAMES HAD REACHED HER COURTYARD LONG BEFORE *WE* COULD.

GOT SOME OF THE OTHER SLEEPERS OUT, THOUGH. THERE WERE *SEVERAL* POCKETS IN THE CITY OUR RESCUE TEAM GOT TO BEFORE THE FIRE DID.

WHO? ANYONE IMPORTANT TO US?

I'M NOT SURE. WE'LL BE DAYS SORTING THEM OUT.

BEST BE ABOUT IT, THEN. IF THE SLEEPING BEAUTY *IS* DEAD, IT'S FEASIBLE THE CURSE DIED WITH HER.

SOME OF THOSE WE RESCUED MAY BE WAKING SOON. LET'S SALVAGE WHAT WE CAN FROM THIS DISASTER.

It took an army of administrators, bureaucrats, clerics and sorcerers to run an empire that spanned worlds, gathered all in one place.

TOO MANY EGGS IN ONE *BASKET*, IF YOU ASK ME.

FUNNY.

THAT WAS *IRONY*, RIGHT?

It's estimated by some that nearly a million souls fell under Briar Rose's spell of endless slumber.

WE SHOULD THINK ABOUT MOVING ON, GUYS.

THERE'LL BE NO MORE PICKINGS HERE.

Less than a thousand of them were brought out alive, when the Sleeping City burned.

WHERE TO THEN, PORKY PINE?

SOME SMALL VILLAGE IN THE COUNTRY, I THINK. A PLACE WHERE TRUSTING FOLKS STILL PUT UNGUARDED *PIES* OUT ON THE WINDOWSILL TO COOL.

Most historians agree that this day marked the final death rattle of the Old Empire.

IT'S ALWAYS ABOUT PIES WITH YOU TWO.

NEED TO SATISFY OUR SWEET TOOTH SOMEHOW, MR. GINGER.

OTHERWISE WE MIGHT HAVE TO SETTLE FOR *GINGER-BREAD*.

BARBARIANS.

I'VE FALLEN AMONG BARBARIANS.

NEXT: WHO WILL INHERIT THE WIND?

FABLES

03

WILLINGHAM · BUCKINGHAM · LEIALOHA

BROCK
BLUEHEART

RAPUNZEL

WEREWOLF
MAN

W

W

①

②

PROFESSOR F

THE GREEN WITCH

REAR VIEW OF
COSTUME

BROCK BLUEHEART

ABLE TO CREATE ARMOR
AND WEAPONS FROM BLUE
CULT FAITH MAGIC.

COSTUME STRAPS
EXPAND AS HE
GROWS

WERE
WOLF
MAN

THE GOLDEN KNIGHT

THUMBELINA

THE
GREEN
WITCH

OZMA

NORTH

BIG BAD WOLF : AKA
WEREWOLF MAN